Understanding Your
Suicide Grief

Also by Alan Wolfelt

*Healing A Child's Grieving Heart: 100 Practical Ideas
for Families, Friends & Caregivers*

*Healing A Friend's Grieving Heart: 100 Practical Ideas
for Helping Someone You Love Through Loss*

*Healing A Teen's Grieving Heart: 100 Practical Ideas for
Families, Friends & Caregivers*

Healing Your Grieving Heart: 100 Practical Ideas

The Journey Through Grief: Reflections on Healing

*Living in the Shadow of the Ghosts of Grief:
Step Into the Light*

*The Understanding Your
Suicide Grief Journal*

*The Understanding Your Suicide
Grief Support Group Guide*

*The Wilderness of Suicide Grief:
Finding Your Way*

Companion
P R E S S

Companion Press is dedicated to the education and support
of both the bereaved and bereavement caregivers. We believe
that those who companion the bereaved by walking with them
as they journey in grief have a wondrous opportunity: to help
others embrace and grow through grief—and to lead fuller, more
deeply-lived lives themselves because of this important ministry.

For a complete catalog and ordering information, write or call:

Companion Press
The Center for Life and Loss Transition
3735 Broken Bow Road
Fort Collins, Colorado 80526
(970) 226-6050

www.centerforloss.com

Understanding Your Suicide Grief

Ten Essential Touchstones for Finding Hope and Healing Your Heart

Alan D. Wolfelt, Ph.D.

Companion
P R E S S

Fort Collins, Colorado
An imprint of the Center for Loss and Life Transition

Companion Press is an imprint of the Center for Loss and Life Transition, 3735 Broken Bow Road, Fort Collins, Colorado 80526.

Printed in the United States of America.

21 20 19 18 17   10 9 8 7 6 5

ISBN: 978-1-879651-58-6

I dedicate this book in memory of my good friend, Ken Frazier, and to the people who have invited me to walk with them through the wilderness of suicide grief. Thank you for transforming your pain into wisdom that helps your fellow strugglers. What you have taught me is contained in the pages of this book. Thank you for entrusting me with your stories of love and loss.

Ken Frazier
June 1, 1946-November 9, 1992

Contents

Foreword

Suicide is death by just another name, but the implications and stigma that surround its mystery and aftermath are strong enough to touch every facet of our lives and of society. It doesn't just seek out the deceitful, the poor, the irresponsible, or the desperate. It happens to those with fulfilling careers—to professionals, physicians, and clergy. It is steadily increasing among the elderly and our sick. It happens to the child, the sibling, the father or mother, the spouse, the provider, the soul-mate, and the best friend. It spans the width and breadth of our population, crossing cultures and manipulating the sliding scale from the young to the old. Suicide knows no boundaries.

Suicide sneaks into our lives, disabling the survivors, who spend the rest of their lives adjusting to the residual taboo. Surviving family and friends typically face social and spiritual dilemmas. It imposes limitations on the lives we once lived as we deal with the pain. We become silent and search aimlessly for peace.

My husband, Gary, and I have lived through the chaos of suicide and struggled, like so many others, to rebuild our lives and step out of the shadows of grief.

During a surprise spring blizzard in April 1993, our son, Chad, took his life in a random, unplanned moment of anger and despair. Our lives changed forever. Outside our window, Gary and I noted how ironic it was that nature echoed this moment in time. Cherry tree branches hung heavily on newly budding trees—one of the first signs of spring in Wisconsin. Branches were bent, close to breaking, as they struggled against the blow of Mother Nature's cruel act. Blinding, swirling snow obscured our vision of what was yet to be. We were frozen in time.

Even the early dawn of a new day couldn't erase the feelings of incredible loss and disbelief we felt. Each bud twinkled with crystal brightness at the first glint of light, just like our never-ending tears. How odious this scene seemed in the face of our sudden loss.

Then, ten weeks later, when the healing rays of sun and the beauty of June were just starting to warm our lives again, Chad's fiancé, Jenny, took her life too. Quite different from Chad's death, Jenny's was planned and executed with precision and intent. In an instant, our arduous path became more complicated and even more painful.

Now the comfort of family and friends who were there during the initial days and months of grief was not enough to sustain us at this point. The trauma of suicide reduced our capacity to accept the demands of everyday life. We lost our connection with who we once were. We were challenged by the unique stigma and complications of death by suicide.

Fortunately, we had the privilege to meet Dr. Alan Wolfelt and share our journey through grief. He helped us rediscover the sanctity of life. This book is a testimony that describes many of the challenges we've faced and overcome. If Dr. Wolfelt's book on suicide had been available years ago, perhaps our journey would have been easier to navigate. At the time, there was no explanation or plan of self-care for such profound grief. In fact, society did little to acknowledge and comfort those affected. One was expected to "carry on" and return to "normal" lives in reasonably short periods of time. We knew we needed to do something with our grief, but we didn't know how to begin.

In this book, Dr. Wolfelt gently teaches the reader how to begin. He explains the normal reactions to death by suicide, never judging, never preaching, but always offering simple gifts of hope through his words. He addresses the misconceptions about grief and death by suicide, such as: only a crazy person completes suicide; suicide is inherited; and no one can help you with your grief. He teaches us how to live in a society where others don't know what to say to us, and we don't know what to say to others.

In the words of Alla Bozarth-Campbell, "Pain is bearable when we are able to trust that it won't last forever, not when we pretend it doesn't exist." Dr. Wolfelt encourages us not to deny, but to present and explore every dimension of raw pain until we've exhausted our need to do so. He admonishes us to be patient, so we are not overwhelmed with the intensity of our grief. And, as we explore, we will find hope and trust in believing this pain will not last forever.

You will feel invited to accept the power of companionship. In this book, Dr. Wolfelt manages to make you feel as though you are walking hand-in-hand with someone who understands your experience and can relate to your pain. You will find it hard to set the book aside but will accept Dr. Wolfelt's advice to do so, as you kindly "dose" yourself with comforting explanations and strategies for self-care. You might feel as though you want to read the book quickly and skip the actual task of doing your grief work. But, by being active and open to exposing the things that hurt, you will ultimately achieve lasting results.

Through Dr. Wolfelt's sensitivity and gentle choice of words, you will be secure in knowing he is compassionate to the agony of your loss. He teaches you how to work through any raging emotions and honor the pain that may have brought you to the edge of despair. In this book, you will find permission to grieve and mourn. You will want to accept the challenge to honor the life of your loved one. You will find peace in your memories. You will find hope in your tomorrows.

There are volumes written on the subject of suicide, but none are as comprehensive and healing as the messages in this book. Dr. Wolfelt guides us through the path of making sense out of the senseless in our darkest days. When our emotions are exhausted by disbelief, humility, and fear, he draws us safely into the light by helping us understand our human reactions. Dr. Wolfelt suggests that you will grow from your experience—not that you wanted this kind of experience to grow from—but, because of your commitment, you will use it as a catalyst for becoming more aware of your spiritual self and your compassion for others. You can achieve a new inner balance. You can restore dignity, sanity, and peace to your existence. You will once again celebrate the spirit of this loving person who once was a part of you and now lives within you.

Nan & Gary Zastrow

Founders: Wings™-A Grief Education Ministry
Wausau, Wisconsin

Welcome: An Invitation to Open Your Heart

"Take this sorrow onto thy heart, and make it a part of thee, and it shall nourish thee till thou art strong again."

Longfellow

Thank you for picking up *Understanding Your Suicide Grief* and allowing me to companion you on your journey. I, too, have walked this path and realize you have been "torn apart" and, just like me, have some very "special needs."

You are heartbroken, and your entire being literally aches physically, emotionally, and spiritually from the pain of the loss of someone who was precious to you. You may well feel alone, isolated, and dazed. As you slowly read and reflect on the content of this book, I hope and pray that you find some sense of comfort and support.

I discovered that as I wrote this book, the words evolved not from my role as a professional grief therapist but as a fellow "companion" in grief. You see, this book is a fulfillment of one of my hopes: a gathering of some valuable Touchstones into a resource that I believe will make a difference in the lives of my fellow human beings who are walking where I have walked as a survivor of someone to suicide.

My good friend Ken Frazier took his life on November 9, 1992. Ken, an attorney who loved sports more than law (which is one of the many reasons I liked him so much!), ended his life at age 46. He went into a garage, started a car, and died from carbon monoxide poisoning. At that moment, my personal and professional life was transformed forever.

Prior to that day, I had supported many people who had had someone they cared deeply about complete suicide. Yet I was totally humbled in the face of my own loss, and words seemed so inadequate. It took me a long time to realize I would never get to talk about sports or life with Ken again. The great friend whom I had played hours of tennis with, ridden horses bareback on a beach in Mexico with, shared so much laughter with, tailgated with before college football games (he made the best Bloody Marys!), ended on that day and in that place.

The suicide death of a friend or family member is not our choice, yet we are faced with the need to confront our raw and life-changing grief. Yet for a number of reasons, we may not know how or where or if we should express the pain that comes with this profound loss. As you will learn throughout this book, the only way to eventually heal is to mourn. As Helen Keller said, "The only way to the other side is through."

As a result of fear and misunderstanding, many of us as survivors of suicide are often left alone and in silence when we desperately need unconditional support and compassion. As a suicide survivor, I discovered firsthand that we suffer in a variety of ways: one, because we need to mourn the loss of someone significant to the meaning of our life; two, because we have experienced a sudden, usually unexpected traumatic death; and three, because we are often shunned by a society unwilling to enter into the pain of our grief. What we need and deserve is unconditional love, not shame or judgment, either for our feelings or the decision made by our loved one.

I truly hope this book provides you some of the unconditional love you need right now in your life journey. All too many people suffer the trauma of suicide grief in isolation. Yet we all need companions if we are to survive and eventually rekindle our own life force. Again, I hope and pray that this book becomes a reliable companion into and through the ten Touchstones that follow.

THE TEN TOUCHSTONES

This brings us to the concept of the "Touchstones" that I believe you will find helpful in your journey. I have used the concept of Touchstones in the book because it speaks to my heart. By definition, a touchstone is a standard or norm against which to measure something. In this book I describe ten Touchstones, or benchmarks. I explore those Touchstones with you not only because they have seemed to help the survivors of suicide I have companioned as a professional caregiver, but they have been helpful to me in my desire to find renewed meaning and purpose following the death of my friend Ken.

Think of your grief as a wilderness—a vast, mountainous, inhospitable forest. You are in the wilderness now. You are in the midst of unfamiliar and often brutal surroundings. You are cold and tired. You must journey through this wilderness. Yet, as you do so with the help of this resource, remember: go slowly. There are no rewards for speed! Basic wilderness training teaches us, "When you get lost, stay put. Wait and call out for help." As you slowly find your way out of this wilderness experience, you must become acquainted with its terrain and learn to follow the sometimes hard-to-find trail that leads to healing.

In the wilderness of your grief, the Touchstones are your trail markers. They are the signs that let you know you are on the right path. I also like to think of them as "wisdom teachings" that the many people I have supported following a suicide death have taught me.

Those who have gone before you and me have indeed left us many trail markers that show us how they made it through the wilderness of suicide grief. If we look, we will see that they have been gracious enough to pass them on to others who enter this inhospitable wilderness. I feel an obligation to teach what they as fellow travelers have taught me. Again, you and I are not alone. Others have gone before us and discovered the strength not only to survive, but eventually to thrive. From the depths of my being, I believe you can too!

And even when you've become a master journeyer and you know well the terrain of your grief, you will at times feel like you are backtracking and being ravaged by the forces around you. This, too, is the nature of grief after a death to suicide. Complete mastery of a wilderness is not possible. Just as we cannot control the winds and the storms and the beasts in nature, we can never have total dominion over our grief.

"The clearest way into the Universe is through a forest wilderness."

John Muir

But if you do the work of mourning, if you become an intrepid traveler on your journey, if you make use of these ten Touchstones, I promise you that you will find your way out of the wilderness of your grief and you will learn to have renewed meaning and purpose in your precious life.

UNDERSTANDING AS SURRENDERING

The title of this book is *Understanding Your Suicide Grief.* But there is a paradox in the concept of *"understanding"* suicide grief. You see, it is instinctive to want to understand or figure out the "why?" of the suicide of someone we love. Yet it is this very need to totally understand that can get us into trouble. When we are confronted with suicide, we face a mystery. It is not possible to know exactly what goes on in the head and heart of a person before he or she completes suicide—it is a mystery. And, as someone once astutely observed, "Mystery is not something to be explained, it is something to be pondered." The starting point for the instinctive "why?" must be anchored in a confession of mystery.

Sometimes we simply cannot understand the suicide death of someone we have cared about so deeply. Yet we often ask, "Why did this happen?" on the pathway to "How will I survive the reality that it did happen?" Do not shame yourself if you struggle with the "why?"; it is organic, instinctive, and often rooted in wanting back a person whom we valued. But in the end, suicide is an act of solitude. We often cannot understand why a person we care so much about would choose death in this way.

I certainly couldn't understand why my friend Ken chose to die. I didn't understand—I protested as a natural part of my grief. While Ken's death by suicide remains a mystery, I do not care any less about him because of his choice than I would have had the circumstances been different.

I have found that sometimes it is in staying open to the mystery and recognizing that we don't understand and can't control everything that some level of understanding comes. In fact, perhaps it is "standing under" the mysterious experience of suicide grief that provides us with a unique perspective. Maybe only after exhausting an instinctive search for the "why" of suicide can we discover a newly defined "why" for our own lives.

"Being open to your eventual healing is more important than trying to understand the 'why?' of the suicide."

Alan D. Wolfelt

My personal and professional experience suggests that right when you are in the midst of your suicide-survivor grief wilderness experience, some well-intentioned, misinformed person will come along and ask, "Why did he or she complete suicide?" It's not enough that we are often asking this ourselves; those whom I call the "morbidly curious" just feel compelled to ask us this question. While some people can respond to this question with clarity and conviction, most of us find it difficult to answer clearly.

Yes, it's instinctive to ponder the question, but don't think you should have the answer! In my experience, understanding comes when we surrender our need to completely understand (we never will). The grief that suicide brings has its own voice and should not be compromised by our need for complete understanding. Surrender

"A life without surrender is a life without commitment."

Jerry Rubin

can actually help you unleash your capacity to openly mourn. Breathe. Give attention to what you need to give attention to. Hold this mystery in your heart and surround yourself with caring, compassionate companions who sit with you in

9

unconditional love and make no judgment on where you are in the journey. I invite you to surrender to your work of mourning.

AN INVITATION TO BEFRIEND HOPE

Through the experiences of walking with and learning from thousands of suicide survivors (and surviving my own personal walk), I want to emphasize the following truth:

You are not to blame, you can and will survive this wilderness experience, and you do not have to go through this alone.

Yes, you do have special needs and are suffering as you sit in the wound of your loss. Yet you cannot only look forward to healing, you can look forward to going on to eventually enjoy life again.

The contents of this book are anchored in the foundation of hope. Hope is an expectation of a good that is yet to be. It is an expression of the present alive with the possible. It is a belief that healing can and will occur. In honoring the ten Touchstones, you are making an effort to find hope for your continued life. Through intentional mourning, you yourself can be the purveyor of your hope. You create hope in yourself by actively mourning the death and setting your intention to heal.

Sitting in your wound: This is about surrendering to your grief in recognition that the only way to the other side is through. This acknowledges you are willing to do the work that mourning requires. Paradoxically, this befriending of your wound is what eventually restores your life and your living. To do this requires that you do not shut the world out, but let the world come in.

When you feel hopeless, frustrated, and are struggling (and you no doubt will at times), you can also challenge yourself to reach out to others for help. Spend time with others who have walked this walk and who affirm your need to mourn yet at the same time give you hope for healing. People

"Whatever enlarges hope will also exalt courage."

Samuel Johnson

who are empathetic, nonjudgmental, good listeners and who
model positive, optimistic ways of being in the world will be
your best companions. They will help resupply you with hope
when your stores are running
low. They will help you build
divine momentum toward
your eventual exodus from the
wilderness of your grief.

*"Hope sees the invisible,
feels the intangible, and
achieves the impossible."*

Anonymous

REMEMBER YOUR HEART

An open heart that is mourning is a well of reception; it is moved
entirely by what it takes in or perceives. Authentic mourning
means being totally vulnerable to what you think and feel in
response to the suicide death. Keeping your heart open wide
allows you to listen to your
life force, or spirit, and slowly
brings you out of the dark and
into the light.

*"The centerpiece of the
integration of grief is not
the mind, but the heart."*

Alan D. Wolfelt

You see, I have learned through
experience that integrating
suicide grief into our lives is heart-based, not head-based. The
contents of this book encourage you to think, yes, but more
importantly to *feel* with all of your heart and soul.

THE COURAGE TO FEEL YOUR FEELINGS OF LOSS

The word *courage* comes from an Indo-European root that
means heart (coeur). When you're impacted so deeply by a
suicide death, part of you may want to shut down your feelings
or try to go around them, inhibit them, or deny them the attention
they demand. The death of someone to suicide pries open your
heart even if it wants to stay closed. Now, as hard as it is to
do, you must open your heart, which has been engaged against
its will, and muster the courage to encounter a wide range of
feelings.

The word *feeling* originates from the Indo-European root and
means "touch." Obviously, all of us are invited to be touched by

11

experiences we encounter along life's path—happy, sad, and everything in between. There is actually a fancy-sounding word called *perturbation* that means when we openly feel our feelings, we discover the capacity to experience change and movement.

"To integrate your grief into your life, you must experience enough safety to feel your feelings."

Alan D. Wolfelt

If you cannot befriend feelings, or if you choose to deny or push them away, you have closed in your ability to use them or be changed by them. Instead of experiencing movement, you become stuck! So, to integrate suicide grief into your life requires that you be touched by what you feel.

Courage also involves doing what you believe is right, despite the fact that others may strongly or persuasively disagree. For example, some of your family and friends may tell you things like, "You need to put the past in the past and move on." Instead, you have had the courage to pick up this book in an effort to better understand your special needs related to being a suicide survivor. Thank you for your courage. Do not allow anyone to deny you your need to authentically mourn.

"Life shrinks or expands in proportion to one's courage."

Anais Nin

This book, directed from my heart to your heart, is an invitation to go to that spiritual place inside yourself and, transcending our mourning-avoidant society (which often misunderstands and ignores suicide grief), enter deeply, but with self-compassion and patience, into the journey. In many ways, the path of the heart is an individual exploration into the wilderness, along unmarked and unlit paths. In part, my hope in this book is to provide you some light along your path.

"Light is known to exist by the virtue of darkness. One is the chair upon which the other sits."

Anonymous

WHAT THIS BOOK IS ABOUT AND HOW TO USE IT

This book will attempt to compassionately invite you to learn about your journey into and through the grief that comes with being a suicide survivor. As you have without doubt already discovered, grief is an intensely personal experience. Your own grief is unlike anyone else's, even though you will find you share many commonalities with others in grief. I hope you discover this book to be a safe place to embrace what you uniquely think and feel without fear of being judged.

As a suicide survivor, you have experienced a trauma loss. Trauma can be defined as an event of such intensity or magnitude that it would overwhelm any human being's capacity to cope with the demands of life. You have been traumatized by the sudden, self-inflicted death of a family member, a friend, a coworker, a neighbor, or someone else whose life touched yours. I do not want you to experience this alone or in isolation.

How is this grief different than your response to an anticipated death? As you know, the death of those we care deeply about naturally results in painful feelings of loss and grief. But when you are faced with a suicide death, your mind has an especially difficult time acknowledging and absorbing the circumstances of the death itself.

In part, the word trauma refers to intense feelings of shock, fear, anxiety, and helplessness surrounding the cause of death. The traumatic nature of suicide and your thoughts and feeling about it will color every aspect of your grief. It is part of your grief. But it is not the totality of your grief.

Trauma: An injury; something hurtful. The wounding of your emotions, your spirit, your beliefs about yourself and the world around you, your will to live, your dignity, your sense of safety and security.

Other factors that I will explore with you in this book include the nature of the relationship you had with the person who completed suicide, your unique personality, your spiritual/religious and cultural background, your gender, your age, your personal experiences with loss, as well as others. So, while there are many things that shape your grief, you can take a proactive role in your eventual healing from this trauma. (In part, you are doing just that by picking up this book.)

By actively engaging with this book, you are empowering yourself to *do* something with your grief—to mourn it, to express it outside of yourself, to find ways to help yourself heal. And you *will* heal. You *will* love and live again. Keep telling yourself, "I am not alone." Millions of others have not only survived a suicide death of a loved one, they've chosen to truly live. Find ways to reach out to these people. Find ways to share your experience. Find ways to make connections.

One way to make a connection is to interact with this book. The companion journal to this book (*The Understanding Your Suicide Grief Journal: Exploring the Ten Essential Touchstones*) gives you needed space to write out your thoughts and feelings. Neither this book nor the journal attempt to prescribe how you should feel but instead invite

> *"Grief waits on welcome, not on time."*
> Alan D. Wolfelt

you to think and feel. While they do describe the ten essential Touchstones, you will find that each of these Touchstones will be lived and experienced in different ways by different people.

This book and journal can also be used in conjunction with a support group. I believe that many people benefit from participation in a support group. To assist in the creation of the group, there is a resource that is part of this series entitled *The Understanding Your Suicide Grief Support Group Guide*. The American Association of Suicidology (www.suicidology.org) and the American Foundation for Suicide Prevention (www.afsp.org) maintain a list of survivor support groups throughout the United States and Canada.

The Language of Suicide

The words we use in referring to suicide are so important. They reflect our values. As we have learned more about being sensitive and compassionate to survivors of suicide, we have seen an important movement to use the word "complete" instead of "commit" to describe the act. This is because the word "commit" has been historically tied to the taboo and stigma surrounding suicide. In addition, the word "commit" is often associated with sin. Additional preferred terms for "commit" are "died by suicide," "killed himself," "took his life," or "suicided."

Still, I realize that the phrase "completed suicide" can also be problematic. Some people think it implies that there were multiple suicide attempts that preceded the actual death, and, as you know, this is often not the case.

The term "survivor" as used in this book refers to a person who experiences the death of a family member or friend to suicide. Some people get confused by this and think it means a person who has attempted suicide but survived. Actually, a person who attempts but does not complete suicide is referred to as an "attempter" or a "survivor of a suicide attempt." I realize that some people do not like the term "suicide survivor," but for the sake of brevity and clarity, I chose to use it in this book. Perhaps it will help you to think of it this way: Someone you love has died, and you are now on a journey to learn how to survive the loss. You are a survivor. In fact, if you do your grief work and receive the support you need, you will not only survive, you will go on to live a life of love and meaning.

The bottom line is that when talking about the death, you should use language that feels comfortable for you. Different people will be comfortable with different language. What feels right to you?

For many survivors, it takes months and even years to acknowledge that the death was by suicide, and during this time of reckoning, you may simply be uncomfortable with ANY language that connotes that the person you love took his or her own life. I understand that. I also know that part of your eventual healing involves fully acknowledging this painful reality, in your head as well as your heart. Whether you use the term "suicide" or the phrases "took his own life," "ended his own life," "killed himself," or "suicided," growing to accept the reality of the means of the death, and being able to admit this reality in the language you use, are essential steppingstones on your journey through the wilderness of suicide grief.

This book is not intended to replace either a support group or personal counseling. No book, not this book or any other book, can ever replace the actual experience of moving your grief into mourning with companions who have walked the walk. No book can replace counseling for those who need it. Seeking counseling for this trauma loss is never a sign of weakness; actually, it is a sign of strength.

I do need to acknowledge that this book is about you, the survivor of a suicide, rather than about those who completed suicide. This is not a book about the "whys" of suicide. While I will explore the instinctive need to ask "why?" as part of the journey, I do not review the various explanations or motivations for suicide. Actually, detailed investigations of the factors that can lead to suicide demonstrate that there are many reasons people take their own lives. Suicide often has multiple determinants. That is, it is the result of a number of factors coming together in a fatal mixture. Often, these determinants may be masked or unknown to family members and friends. In fact, they may not even be visible to the person who ended his or her own life.

Having said this, I do encourage you to complete the companion journal, whether you do it on your own, in conjunction with a support group based on this book, or with a professional counselor. Journaling your experience is a powerful means for helping you with your grief. Use this book and the journal fully. When you read or reflect on a section that really speaks to you or gives you a new insight, highlight it and come back to it. You may be amazed at how helpful it can be to create a time to talk about these meaningful sections with a trusted friend, a compassionate counselor, or a safe support group.

Finally, I want to acknowledge that this book may be difficult for you to read and process. As you read the chapters that follow, allow yourself the time you need to fully engage with the words and the meaning. Reading too much in one sitting may be overwhelming. If this is the case for you, allow yourself to read short passages then set the book aside to come back to later. If you encounter discussions that seems too painful to explore

17

right now, skip over those passages. Just as you need to dose yourself with your grief, you may also need to dose yourself with the content of this book. And if and when this book stirs painful and difficult feelings within you, find a compassionate, nonjudgmental friend to share them with.

REACH OUT TO YOUR FELLOW SURVIVORS

I cannot emphasize enough how in my experience it is in the companionship of our fellow survivors of suicide that we often find solace and support. As survivors we know not to judge each other. As survivors we share the same language. As survivors we can acknowledge any regrets openly and without shame. As survivors we can describe the actual act, no matter how traumatic, and, no, we won't be blamed for the death. As survivors we can honor our need to mourn in ways that are not based on speculation or gossip. As survivors we can go on to live fully until we die!

"The quality and quantity of understanding support you get as you mourn a suicide death will have a major influence on your capacity to not only heal, but to eventually transcend. You cannot—nor should you try to—do this alone. Drawing on experiences and encouragement of friends, counselors, and fellow travelers of this experience is not a weakness, but rather a healthy human need."

Alan D. Wolfelt

BELIEVE IN YOUR CAPACITY TO HEAL

Yes, your life has been turned upside down by this suicide. You are faced with re-creating yourself as you search for the "new you." You didn't ask for this challenge to your capacity to survive this tragedy. You are not the same person you were before the suicide. Your "divine spark"—that which gives your life meaning and purpose—has been muted. Yet, all of the survivors of suicide I have had the privilege of meeting and learning from want me to tell you this: *you will survive*. You may think you cannot get through this, but you can and you will. Yes, you need to have the intention to sit in the wound, but over time and with the love and support of others, your grief will soften and you will find ways to be happy again. There will come a day when this suicide death is not the first thing you think of when you wake up each morning. As you do your hard work of mourning, you can and will choose not to simply survive, but to truly live.

IN GRATITUDE

I thank those of you who have invited me to walk with you in the wilderness of suicide grief. Thank you for transforming your pain into wisdom and your darkness into light. What you have taught me I hope to teach others in the pages of this book. Thank you for entrusting me with your stories of love and loss.

To the reader, I hope this book brings you hope, wisdom, and grace. Hope, wisdom, and grace are qualities of the soul. They invite us to engage deeply with our fellow human beings and the world around us.

HOPE is the promise that you will survive and go on to find continued meaning and purpose in your life. When your pain seems unbearable, hope allows you to sit in your wound yet hold in your heart an expectation of a good that is yet to be.

WISDOM is the soul's intelligence delivered from those who have walked this walk before you. Open your heart to these sources of wisdom and allow them to surprise you. You will probably discover that help comes from unlikely sources.

GRACE is what eases the way, softens the wound, cushions the sorrow, and lightens the burden. Grace allows for the transformation of your grief, the nourishment of your spirit, and ultimately the illumination of your soul.

When you cultivate hope, wisdom, and grace, you will be invited to envision a larger world, a world of breathtaking beauty alive with the potential of renewal, and the power and the glory to invite you to live again, never forgetting those who have gone before you.

If you find this book helpful, please drop me a note (3735 Broken Bow Road, Fort Collins, CO 80526) or email me (DrWolfelt@centerforloss.com) about your journey and allow me to learn from you. Again, I thank you from deep in my soul for having the courage to explore the Touchstones I have provided in this resource. I hope we meet one day!

Alan D. Wolfelt, Ph.D., C.T.
Director, Center for Loss & Life Transition
Fort Collins, Colorado

Touchstone One

Open to the Presence of Your Loss

"In every heart there is an inner room, where we can hold our greatest treasures and our deepest pain."

Marianne Williamson

Someone you love has completed suicide. In your heart, you have come to know your deepest pain. To be "bereaved" literally means "to be torn apart." You have a broken heart and your life has been turned upside down.

From my own experience with the death of a close friend to suicide, as well as my experience of supporting hundreds of survivors over the years, I have learned that we cannot go around the pain that is the wilderness of grief. Instead, we must journey all through it, sometimes shuffling along the less strenuous side paths, somctimcs plowing dircctly into the center.

While it is instinctive to want to run as far away as possible from the overwhelming pain that comes with this loss, you have probably already discovered that even if you try to hide, deny, or self-treat your pain, it is still within you, demanding your attention. In acknowledging the inevitability of the pain and raw suffering that comes with this grief, in coming to understand the need to gently embrace the pain, you in effect honor the pain. "What?" you naturally protest. "Honor the pain?" As strange as it may sound, your pain is the key that opens your heart and ushers you on your way to eventual healing.

In many ways, this book is about helping you face the pain of your loss so you can enter into and through your darkness and come into the light. The word *honor* literally means recognizing the value of and respecting. It is not instinctive to see grief that erupts following a suicide death and the need to mourn as something to honor. I certainly didn't want to honor my pain when my friend Ken took his life. However, I discovered that it was necessary and ultimately healing. I hope you discover as I did that to honor (value it, respect it, give it the attention it demands) your grief is not self-destructive or harmful, it is self-sustaining and life-giving.

What is Healing in Grief?

To heal in grief is to become whole again, to integrate your grief into yourself, and to learn to continue your changed life with fullness and meaning. Experiencing a new and changed "wholeness" requires that you engage in the work of mourning. It doesn't *happen* to you; you must stay open to that which has broken you.

Healing is a holistic concept that embraces the physical, emotional, cognitive, social, and spiritual realms. Note that healing is not the same as curing, which is a medical term that means "remedying" or "correcting." You cannot correct your grief, but you can heal it.

You have probably been taught that pain is an indication that something is wrong and that you should find a way to alleviate the pain. In our culture, pain and feelings of loss are experiences most people try to avoid. Why? Because the role of pain and suffering is misunderstood. This is particularly true with suicide grief. Because of the stigma and taboo surrounding suicide, many people think you shouldn't talk about it, let alone honor your pain by openly mourning. Normal thoughts and feelings after a suicide death are still seen by some as unnecessary, even inappropriate.

You will learn over time, if you haven't already, that the pain of suicide grief will keep trying to get your attention until you have the courage to gently, and in small doses, open to its presence. The alternatives—denying, suppressing, or self-treating your pain—are in fact more painful.

I have learned that the pain that surrounds the closed heart of grief is the pain of living against yourself, the pain of denying how the loss changed you, the pain of feeling alone and isolated—unable to openly mourn, unable to love and be loved by those around you. Denied grief results in what I term "living in the shadow of the ghosts of grief" (see my book by this title for an outline of the consequences of carrying your pain), which is a state in which you essentially die while you are still alive.

Taboo: something society decides is so terrible that no one is allowed to do it, talk about it, or learn about it.

Stigma: the mark of shame and ridicule placed on those people who do kill themselves, and on their families. The stigma is the punishment for breaking the taboo.

People are often anxious and afraid of what they do not understand, so this stigma exists because of fear. So, sad to say you will have to reach out and find safe, nonjudgmental people who support your need to mourn openly and honestly.

Instead of dying while you are alive, you can choose to allow yourself to remain open to the pain. Paradoxically, it is gathering courage to move toward the pain that ultimately leads to the healing of your wounded heart. Your integrity is engaged by your feelings and the commitment you make to honor the truth in them.

In part, this book will encourage you to be present to your multitude of thoughts and feelings, to "be with" them, for they contain the truth you are searching for, the energy you may be lacking, and the unfolding of your eventual healing. While it can be tempting to only want to allow a limited range of feelings to surface, my experience suggests you will need all of your thoughts and feelings to lead you there, not just the feelings you find acceptable. For it is in being honest with yourself that you find your way through the wilderness and identify the places that need to be healed.

EXPRESS YOURSELF: Go to *The Understanding Your Suicide Grief Journal* on p. 10.

STAYING PRESENT TO YOUR PAIN

As you stay present to your pain that comes with the experience of suicide survivor grief, you will be participating in "soul work," which will eventually lead to "spirit work". Keep in mind that "soul work" precedes "spirit work."

Soul Work: A downward movement in the psyche; a willingness to connect with what is dark, deep, and not necessarily pleasant.

Spirit Work: A quality of moving toward the light; upward ascending.

"A wound that goes unacknowledged and unwept is a wound that cannot heal."

John Eldredge

In part, healing and transcendence are about your willingness to descend into your soul work on the path to your spirit work. My personal and professional experience suggests that when we experience the death of someone we care deeply about to suicide, we must allow ourselves to descend before we can transcend.

EXPRESS YOURSELF: Go to *The Understanding Your Suicide Grief Journal* on p. 11.

SETTING YOUR INTENTION TO HEAL

You are on a journey that is naturally frightening, painful, and often lonely. No words, written or spoken, can take away the pain you feel now. I hope, however, that this book will bring you some comfort and encouragement as you make a commitment to embracing that very pain.

It takes a true commitment to heal in your grief. Yes, you are wounded, but with commitment and intention you can and will become whole again. Commitment goes hand in hand with the concept of "setting your intention." Intention is defined as being conscious of what you want to experience. A close cousin to "affirmation," it is using the power of positive thought to produce a desired result.

"Much of the pain from suicide grief can come from trying to keep the pain secret."
Alan D. Wolfelt

How can this concept of setting intention influence your journey through grief? When you set your intention to heal, you make a true commitment to positively influence the course of your journey. You choose between

"You need to have the intention to survive, and if you don't have the tools, you have to reach out for them."
Iris Bolton

what I call being a "passive witness" or an "active participant" in your grief. You have probably heard or been told the cliché: "Time heals all wounds." Yet, time alone has nothing to do with healing the wounds of grief that come with suicide. I like to remind myself and other survivors that healing waits on welcome, not on time! Healing and integrating this loss into your life demands that you engage actively in the grief journey. It can't be fixed or resolved; it can only be soothed and "integrated" or "reconciled" through actively experiencing the multitude of thoughts and feelings involved.

EXPRESS YOURSELF: Go to *The Understanding Your Suicide Grief Journal* on p. 11.

INTEGRATING YOUR SUICIDE GRIEF

The concept of intention-setting presupposes that your outer reality is a direct reflection of your inner thoughts and beliefs. If you can change or mold some of your thoughts or beliefs, then you can influence your reality. In journaling and speaking (and praying!) your intentions, you can help set them.

You might tell yourself, "I can and will reach out for support during this difficult time in my life. I can and will find people who do not change the subject or feel a need to run away when I tell my story. I will look to people who can accept the new person I have become. I will become filled with hope that I can and will survive this tragic death."

Setting your intention as in the above example is not only a way of helping yourself heal (although it is indeed that!), it is a way of actively guiding your grief. Of course, you will still have to honor and embrace your pain during this time. By honoring the presence of your pain, by understanding the appropriateness of your pain, you are committing to facing the pain. You are committing to paying attention to your experience in ways that allow you to eventually begin to breathe life into your soul again. What better reason to give attention to your intention!

Integration or Reconciliation

An important concept to keep in mind as you journey through grief is that of integration or reconciliation. You cannot get over or resolve your grief, but you can integrate or reconcile yourself to it. That is, you can learn to incorporate your grief into your consciousness and re-discover meaning and purpose in your life. See Touchstone Nine for more on integration and reconciliation.

 In reality, denying your grief, running from it, or minimizing it only seems to make it more confusing and overwhelming. Paradoxically, to eventually soften your heart, you must embrace your grief. As strange as it may seem, you must make it your friend.

In this book, I will attempt to teach you to gently and lovingly befriend your grief. To not be ashamed to express it. To not be ashamed of your tears and profound feelings of sadness. To try not to pull down the blinds that shut out light and love. Slowly and in doses, you can and will return to life and begin to live in ways that put stars back into your sky.

A Survivor Speaks:

"Once I decided I wanted to go on living, I committed myself to facing what I had to face. It's been so hard, but it has been more than worth it."

EXPRESS YOURSELF: Go to *The Understanding Your Suicide Grief Journal* on p. 12.

NO REWARD FOR SPEED

Reconciling your grief does not happen quickly or efficiently. The grief work surrounding suicide may be some of the hardest work you ever do. Because grief is work, it naturally leaves you feeling drained. That is why you probably are experiencing what is called the "lethargy of grief," where you don't feel like you have any physical, emotional, or spiritual energy. Can you relate?

Consequently, you must be patient with yourself. When you come to trust the pain will not last forever, it becomes tolerable. Deceiving yourself into thinking the pain does not even exist is sure to make it intolerable. Spiritual maturity in your grief work is attained when you embrace a paradox: to live at once in the state of both encounter and surrender, to both "work at" and "surrender to" your grief.

As you come to know this paradox, you will slowly discover the soothing of your soul. Resist the need to figure out everything with your head, and let the paradox embrace you. You will find yourself wrapped in a gentle peace—the peace of living at once in both *encounter* (feeling the pain of your

Dosing Your Pain

While this first Touchstone seeks to help you understand the role of pain in your healing and eventual transcendence, I want to make sure you also understand that you cannot embrace the pain of your suicide grief all at once. If you were to feel it all at once, you would no doubt feel overwhelmed and unsure that you could survive. Instead, you must allow yourself to "dose" the pain—feel it in small waves then allow yourself to retreat until you are ready for the next wave.

grief) and *surrender* (embracing the mystery without trying to "understand" it with your head).

A Survivor Speaks:

"At first, I couldn't even get my feet out of the bed. It was a major accomplishment to take a shower. I would say with my head, 'Get going,' but my body said, 'You aren't going anywhere.'"

Understanding the Concept of Surrender

The concept of surrender teaches you that when you stop resisting and surrender to your situation exactly as it is, things begin to change. Resistance is an instinctive defense mechanism you use to push away or deny your pain to protect you from your feelings of loss and grief. In the end, resistance robs you of your capacity to heal and transcend. When you surrender, you acknowledge, "This is what I am faced with right now in my life's journey (the suicide death of someone dear to me). While I'd like it to be different, I must allow myself to face the reality of what is happening." When you surrender, you release attachment to how you feel your life *should* be and invite yourself to be in the presence of your life *exactly as it is*. While naturally difficult to do, surrender is an act of courage.

EXPRESS YOURSELF: Go to *The Understanding Your Suicide Grief Journal* on p. 13.

A VITAL DISTINCTION: SHOCK VERSUS DENIAL

Shock along with elements of denial is a temporary, healthy response that essentially says, "The reality of the suicide death of someone dear to me is too painful to acknowledge right now.

Therefore I refuse to believe it." *While this is a natural initial reaction to suicide, you will hinder your eventual healing if you stay in long-term denial.*

There are various forms of denial that, as a survivor, you must work to break through:

Conscious Denial: This is where you hide the fact that the death was suicide. You may tell people it was a heart attack, murder, or an unexplained sudden death.

Innocent Denial: This is where you hold onto the hope that the findings that ruled the death a suicide were a mistake and will be changed at a later date.

Blame as Denial: This is where you blame someone else for the suicide, thereby denying the choice someone made to take his or her own life.

Pretense and Denial: This is where the family rule is that you never talk about the death or use the word suicide at any time.

The various motivations for these forms of denial are often multiple and complex. Often, people don't even realize they are in denial. So, if you discover you have gone beyond shock into some form of prolonged denial, do not shame or ridicule yourself.

But here is the problem: By staying in whatever form of denial, you miss the opportunity to do the grief work related to your feelings. You inhibit your capacity to experience perturbation (see p. 70). As you have seen emphasized in this chapter, befriending your pain is central to your ultimate healing. Until denial is broken through and the pain is experienced, you are on hold and authentic mourning cannot take place. If you find yourself stuck in denial, commit yourself to working on this first and foremost. There is good reason that I address this in Touchstone One of this book. Why? Because until you break through denial, the additional Touchstones that follow do you little good. Of course, if you were in long-term denial, you probably would not be reading this book. Odds are you probably know some family members and friends who will not read this book, preferring to maintain their personal denial.

A Survivor Speaks:

"I went from shock into denial and stayed there for a long time. Ultimately, I discovered I was becoming my own worst enemy. Fortunately, I found a compassionate counselor who gently led the way and invited me to face the reality of the suicide of my son. That is when my mourning really started."

EXPRESS YOURSELF: Go to *The Understanding Your Suicide*

A SPECIAL CAUTION

You may have some people in your family or friendship system who totally refuse to acknowledge that the cause of death was suicide. You must overcome any instinct to think your role is to convince them that the death was a suicide. Forcing them to confront the facts is insensitive and dangerous. Some people stay in denial for long periods of time, some even until their own deaths. Be patient and kind. You are responsible *to* people, not *for* them. What I as a therapist might do to help someone gently confront the reality of suicide is very different than you confronting a family member or friend.

Grief Journal on p. 14.

FACE ANY INAPPROPRIATE EXPECTATIONS

You are at risk for having inappropriate expectations about this death. These expectations result from common societal messages that tell you to "be strong" in the face of life losses. Invariably, some well-intentioned people around you will urge you to "move on," "let go," "keep your chin up," and "keep busy." Actually, you need to give yourself as much time as you need to mourn, and these kinds of comments hurt you, not help you.

Often combined with these messages is an unstated but strong belief that you have a right not to hurt, so do whatever you can to avoid it. The unfortunate result is that you may be encouraged by

"It doesn't matter how slowly you go as long as you do not stop."

Confucius

some people to be happy when you need to be sad, to self-treat your pain in some way, or to deny your profound feelings of loss and grief.

Society often tends to make those of us in grief feel shame or embarrassment about our feelings of grief, particularly suicide grief. Shame can be described as the feeling that something you are doing is bad. And you may feel that if you mourn, then you should be ashamed. If you are perceived as "doing well," you are often seen as "being strong" and "under control." The message is that the well-controlled person stays rational at all times. (See more on embarrassment on p. 93.)

Combined with this message is another one. Society erroneously implies that if you, as a grieving person, openly express your feeling of grief, you are being immature. If your feelings are fairly intense, you may be labeled overly emotional or needy. If your feelings are extremely intense, you may even be referred to as crazy or a "pathological mourner."

As a professional grief counselor, I assure you that you are not immature, overly emotional, or crazy. But the societal messages surrounding grief that you may receive are! I often say that society has it backwards in defining who is "doing well" in grief and who is "not doing well."

From an early age, you may have been taught to conceal emotions, particularly emotions like sadness, anxiety, and depression. You may have learned to put on a happy face and to have a stiff upper lip. Perhaps you were even exposed to the saying, "Laugh and the world laughs with you; weep and you weep alone."

If you fear emotions and see them as negative, you will be at risk for crying alone and in private. You will be at risk for trying to run from and hide from some very real, human emotions that try to surface when someone you care about completes suicide. Of course, shame and secrecy then continue.

Yet, being secretive with your emotions doesn't integrate your painful feelings of loss; it complicates them. Then even more pain comes from trying to keep the pain secret. You cannot hide your feelings *and* find renewed meaning in your life. If you are dishonest about your pain, you stay in pain.

Being dishonest with your emotions surrounding this suicide death may temporarily help you get through each day, but it will catch up with you in the end. In essence, you can mourn now or mourn later. You see, the pain of grief is so powerful it will eventually catch up to you. Healing is a process of truth, and you cannot experience truth if you are dishonest with your emotions. If you deny the emotions of your heart, you deny the essence of your life.

"To suppress the grief, the pain, is to condemn oneself to a living death. Living fully means feeling fully; it means being completely one with what you are experiencing and not holding it at arm's length."
David Kaplean

To be open to the presence of your loss, you must accept that you are not wrong to feel what you feel, be it anger, sadness, guilt, fear, whatever. There is no such thing as a negative emotion. If you judge yourself for mourning, you will feel shame. When it comes to healing the wounds of suicide grief, honesty is the best policy.

When you open to the presence of your loss, you will see that no feeling is inherently bad, negative, or wrong. By being honest with yourself and others, the pain you feel begins to soften. It is through being honest that you discover you are not alone and that compassionate people are available to be supportive to you.

A Survivor Speaks:

"At first I thought my feelings meant I was being weak. So I tried to stay strong. But in a support group I learned that my feelings were not out to get me! They were actually trying to tell me to give attention to my need to openly, and without any sense of shame, mourn. Now I have learned to have gratitude for my ability to feel."

EXPRESS YOURSELF: Go to *The Understanding Your Suicide Grief Journal* on p. 15.

GRIEF IS NOT A DISEASE

You have probably already discovered that no quick fix exists for the pain you are enduring. Grief following a suicide is naturally complex, and it is easy to feel overwhelmed. But I promise you that if you can think, feel, and see yourself as an active participant in your healing, you will slowly but surely experience a renewed sense of meaning and purpose in your life.

Grief is not a disease. To be human means coming to know loss as part of your life. Many losses, or "little griefs," occur along life's path. And not all of your losses are as painful as others; they do not always

"We have to do the best we can. This is our sacred responsibility."

Albert Einstein

disconnect you from yourself. But the suicide death of someone you have cared deeply about is likely to leave you feeling disconnected from both yourself and the outside world.

While the grief that accompanies suicide is a powerful, life-changing experience, so, too, is your ability to help facilitate your own healing. In this moment, you are demonstrating your commitment and setting your intention to reinvest in life and living. How? Through your willingness to read and reflect on the pages in this book, complete the companion journal (at your own pace), and participate in a support group with fellow travelers.

I invite you to gently confront the pain of your grief. Be open

33

to the miracle of healing. Integrating the grief that comes with a suicide death requires your willingness. You must have willingness or you would not have picked up this book. Follow your willingness, and allow it to bless you.

In large part, healing from a suicide death is anchored in a decision to not judge yourself but to love yourself. Grief is a call for love. So, if you are judging yourself and where you are in this journey, STOP! Judgment will not free you to mourn, it will only make you afraid to do so. When you stop judging the multitude of emotions that come with your grief, you are left with acceptance, and when you have acceptance (or surrender), you have love. Love will lead you into and through the wilderness, to a place where you will come out of the dark and into the light. Thanks for the opportunity to companion you, and remember: you are not alone!

Be Aware

Some of your previous friends may avoid you or hesitate to talk to you about the person in your life who completed suicide. These behaviors are often a reflection of the stigma that still surrounds suicide. Your capacity to talk openly about it can help reduce the stigma. The key is finding the safe people who will support and nurture you on your journey.

EXPRESS YOURSELF: Go to *The Understanding Your Suicide Grief Journal* on p. 15.

Touchstone Two

Dispel the Misconceptions About Suicide and Grief and Mourning

Misconception: A misconception is a mistaken notion you might have about something—in other words, something you believe to be true but that is not true. Misconceptions about grief are common in our society because we tend not to openly mourn or talk about grief and mourning. You can see how we'd have misconceptions about something as "in the closet" as suicide grief.

As you journey through the wilderness of your suicide grief, if you mourn openly and authentically, you will come to find a path that feels right for you. That is your path to healing. But beware—others may try to pull you off this path. They may try to make you believe that the path you have chosen is wrong— even crazy—and that their way is better.

The reason that people try to pull you from the path is that they have internalized some common misconceptions about suicide grief and mourning. And the misconceptions, in essence, deny you your right to hurt and authentically express your grief. They often cause unrealistic expectations about the grief experience. To integrate this loss into your soul, you must first be willing to unlearn the following misconceptions about suicide and grief and mourning.

As you read about this important Touchstone, you may discover that you yourself have believed in some of the misconceptions and that some may be embraced by people around you. Don't condemn yourself or others for believing in them. They can seem like common sense, and it is also easy to believe something about which you have no actual experience. Simply make use of any new insights you might gain to help you open your heart to your work of mourning in ways that restore your soul.

MISCONCEPTION 1: GRIEF AND MOURNING ARE THE SAME THING.

Perhaps you have noticed that people tend to use the words "grieving" and "mourning" interchangeably. There is an important distinction, however. We as humans move toward integrating loss into our lives not just by grieving, but by mourning. You will move toward reconciliation (see p. 197) not just by grieving, but through active and intentional mourning.

Grief is the constellation of internal thoughts and feelings we have when someone we love dies. Think of grief as the

Bereavement: "to be torn apart," "to have special needs," "to be robbed."

container. It holds all of your thoughts, feelings, and images of your experience when you are bereaved. In other words, grief is the internal meaning given to the experience of loss.

Mourning is when you take the grief you have on the inside and express it outside of yourself. Another way of defining mourning is "grief gone public" or "the outward expression of grief." Talking about the person who died, crying, expressing your thoughts and feelings through art or music, and celebrating special anniversary dates that held meaning for the person who died are just a few examples of mourning.

A major theme of this book is rooted in the importance of openly and honestly mourning the suicide death, in expressing your grief outside of yourself. Over time and with the support of others, to mourn is to heal.

WARNING: After someone you love has died by suicide, your friends may encourage you to keep your grief to yourself. If you were to take this message to heart, the disastrous result would be that all of your thoughts and feelings would stay neatly bottled up inside you. A catalyst for healing, however, can only be created when you develop the courage to mourn publicly, in the presence of understanding, compassionate people who will not judge you. At times, of course, you will grieve alone, but expressing your grief outside of yourself is necessary if you are to slowly and gently move forward in your grief journey.

I think it's so interesting that many native cultures actually create vessels, usually baskets, pots, or bowls, that symbolically contained their grief. They would put these vessels away for periods of time, only to bring them out on a regular basis to help themselves mourn.

Another way to think about what these cultures were instinctively doing was dosing themselves with their grief. As I've said, grief must be embraced little by little, in small bits, with breaks in between. This dosing helps you survive what would, if absorbed in its totality all at once, probably kill you.

When you don't honor a death loss by acknowledging it, first to yourself and then to those around you, the grief will accumulate. Then the denied losses come flowing out in all sorts of potential ways (e.g., deep depression, physical complaints, difficulty in relationships, addictive behaviors), compounding the pain of your loss.

EXPRESS YOURSELF: Go to *The Understanding Your Suicide Grief Journal* on p. 18.

MISCONCEPTION 2: GRIEF FOLLOWING A SUICIDE DEATH ALWAYS RESULTS IN "COMPLICATED" OR "PATHOLOGICAL" MOURNING.

Actually, there is research that indicates that survivors of suicide integrate grief at about the same pace as those who experience any kind of unanticipated death. This misconception could have you believing that you should suffer longer.

This does not mean that a suicide death won't be viewed differently (see the circumstances of death, p. 54). Obviously, there can be some natural challenges, such as the combination of sudden shock, the natural question of "why?", the trauma of witnessing or discovering the suicide, the lack of support from family and friends, and the potential of "secondary victimization" that results from cruel, judgmental, or insensitive comments. Yes, you will have griefbursts (see p. 51) and naturally do some "catch-up" mourning (see p. 131) as you continue with your life, but do not let this misconception become a self-fulfilling prophecy. Do your work of mourning, and you will come out of the dark and into the light.

EXPRESS YOURSELF: Go to *The Understanding Your Suicide Grief Journal* on p. 19.

MISCONCEPTION 3: GRIEF AND MOURNING PROGRESS IN PREDICTABLE, ORDERLY STAGES.

Probably you have already heard about the stages of grief. This type of thinking about dying, grief, and mourning is appealing but inaccurate. The notion of stages helps people make sense of death, an experience that is usually not orderly or predictable. If we believe that everyone grieves by going through the same stages, then death and grief become much less mysterious and fearsome. If only it were so simple!

The concept of stages was popularized in 1969 with the publication of Elisabeth Kübler-Ross's landmark text *On Death and Dying*. In this important book, Dr. Kübler-Ross lists the five stages of grief that she saw terminally ill patients experience in the face of their own impending deaths: denial; anger; bargaining; depression;

and acceptance. However, Dr. Kübler-Ross never intended for her stages to be interpreted as a rigid, linear sequence to be followed by all mourners. Readers, however, have done just that, and the consequences have often been disastrous.

As a grieving person, you will probably encounter others who have adopted a rigid system of beliefs about what you should experience in your grief journey. And if you have internalized this

"We have to find ways to unlearn those things that screen us from the perception of profound truth."
Thomas Moore

misconception, you may also find yourself trying to prescribe your grief experience as well. Instead of allowing yourself to be where you are, you may try to force yourself to be in another "stage."

For example, the common responses of disorganization, fear, guilt, and explosive emotions may or may not occur during your unique grief journey. Or relief may occur anywhere along the way and invariably overlap another part of your response. Sometimes your emotions may follow each other within a short period of time; or, at other times, two or more emotions may be present simultaneously. Remember—do not try to determine where you "should" be. Just allow yourself to be naturally where you are in the process.

Everyone mourns in different ways. Personal experience is your best teacher about where you are in your grief journey. Don't think your goal is to move through prescribed stages of grief. As you read further in this book, you will find that a major theme is understanding that your grief is unique. That word means "only one." No one ever existed exactly like you before, and no one will ever be exactly like you again. As part of the healing process, the thoughts and feelings you will experience will be totally unique to you.

EXPRESS YOURSELF: Go to *The Understanding Your Suicide Grief Journal* on p. 20.

MISCONCEPTION 4: WE CAN ALWAYS DETERMINE THE "WHYS?" OF A SUICIDE DEATH.

You may naturally have some of what I like to refer to as psycho-spiritual "why?" questions. You may search for answers, look for clues, and try to make sense of the "why?" of this person's death. Do not punish yourself for this instinctive response to trauma loss. Why did the person do this? can be a painful yet natural question to explore. As a matter of fact, watch out for well-intentioned people who say, "Don't ask why; it doesn't do you any good." Those people often do not understand the normalcy of how "why?" questions precede "how?" questions. "Why did this happen?" is part of the pathway to get yourself to "How will I survive that he or she did this?" Again, do not shame yourself if you find this is part of your journey.

Having acknowledged the normalcy of "why?" questions, detailed investigation of the factors that can lead to a suicide death demonstrate that there are usually many reasons people take their own lives. These signs may be unknown or masked to family members and friends. In fact, they are often not even able to be seen by the person who completes suicide.

So, the misconception is that we always know why, when the reality is we often don't know the specifics of why. My experience with many survivors suggests that you may very slowly, with no rewards for speed, discover that it is possible to live with the uncertainty of never fully knowing the answer to "why?"

EXPRESS YOURSELF: Go to *The Understanding Your Suicide Grief Journal* on p. 21.

MISCONCEPTION 5: ALL SUICIDE SURVIVORS FEEL GUILTY.

The sad reality is that some people will actually say directly to you, "I bet you feel guilty" or pose the question, "Do you feel guilty?" This is one of the most prescribed responses for survivors of suicide. Many books about suicide survivorship give the most coverage to the topic of guilt.

In reality, as a survivor you may or may not feel guilty. Besides, assuming you feel guilt is the opposite of my belief that you are the expert of your own experience and therefore you must teach me what you feel; I must not prescribe what you should feel.

People do not know how you feel unless they give you the opportunity to teach them. People do not automatically assume survivors feel guilty after a death from a heart attack or cancer. Therefore, we should not assume guilt after a suicide death. Many survivors have worked long and hard to help someone prior to a suicide death.

As one astute person noted, "This assumption, from the Dark Ages, that we should have some brand to show people our guilt and shame from having a suicide in the family lives on." So, if you are experiencing guilt, find a safe place with caring people where you can explore it. But, I plead with you, do not assume you have to feel guilty.

EXPRESS YOURSELF: Go to *The Understanding Your Suicide Grief Journal* on p. 22.

MISCONCEPTION 6: ONLY CERTAIN KINDS OF PEOPLE COMPLETE SUICIDE.

This is a simple misconception to dispel. The reality is that suicide is a stranger to no race, creed, religion, age group, income bracket, or socioeconomic level. All kinds of people have completed suicide since the beginning of recorded history.

EXPRESS YOURSELF: Go to *The Understanding Your Suicide Grief Journal* on p. 23.

MISCONCEPTION 7: ONLY A CRAZY PERSON COMPLETES SUICIDE.

While the person you loved who completed suicide may have been depressed, anxious, or hopeless, to be sure, most of us survivors don't find comfort when people try to tell us the person was crazy. Not all suicides meet some formal criteria for mental illness, and even when they do, we don't need to hear that they were crazy.

Related to this, according to the American Association of Suicidology (AAS), approximately two-thirds of people who complete suicide are depressed, and the risk of suicide in people with major depression is about twenty times that of the general population. Depression, often undiagnosed and untreated, is the major cause of suicide.

Again, some people will think they are helping you when they claim your loved one must have been crazy. However, this does not lighten your burden and uplift your spirit. And, it is not a good use of language to assist in your understanding. Even when the person you cared about so deeply had a diagnosable mental illness, we don't need to use the word crazy.

EXPRESS YOURSELF: Go to *The Understanding Your Suicide Grief Journal* on p. 23.

MISCONCEPTION 8: IT IS A SIN TO COMPLETE SUICIDE, AND THE PERSON WHO DOES GOES DIRECTLY TO HELL.

It was not all that long ago that suicide was considered a sin by many of the major bodies of faith. Historically, it was considered by many not just a sin, but an unpardonable sin.

Thank God we now have religious leaders and well-respected theologians who are compassionately and non-judgmentally educating people that suicide is not a sin. As one Catholic priest observed about suicide, "When its victims wake on the other side, they are met by a gentle Christ who stands right inside of their huddled fear and says, 'Peace be with you!' As we see in the gospels, God can go through locked doors, breathe out peace in places where we cannot get in, and write straight with even the most crooked of lines." But watch out for some people who do continue to preach that suicide is a sin. Find people who recognize that faith is about being open to the mystery. I always like to remind myself that "mystery"—the ancient name for God—is something to be pondered, not explained. If someone starts preaching to you that suicide is a sin and that your loved one has gone to hell, get the heck away from him or her as fast as you can.

Personally, I believe there are no limits to God's compassion. God mourns with us. He doesn't send our loved ones to "burn in hell" as someone might try to tell you. If you believe as I do that God's nature is one of steadfast mercy and love, then we realize this is a misconception we need to keep educating the world about.

EXPRESS YOURSELF: Go to *The Understanding Your Suicide Grief Journal* on p. 24.

MISCONCEPTION 9: SUICIDE IS INHERITED AND RUNS IN THE FAMILY.

Be alert for uninformed people who may project to you that because someone in your family completed suicide, you may have the same fate. This projection is not supported by the facts. Scientific research has not at this time confirmed a genetic basis for suicide risk. Please do not listen to people who try to tell you you are doomed to one day complete suicide.

Having acknowledged the obvious, we do know through research that substance abuse disorders, depression disorders, and schizophrenia tend to run in families. However, even if you have family members who have died by suicide after having suffered from these types of disorders, you are not predestined to complete suicide. So, again, do not let anyone tell you that you are.

Instead, if you are just being wise and self-compassionate, you will use this research information to do what you can to reduce your risk. This can include educating yourself about the warning signs related to risk for suicide, not abusing alcohol or drugs, and not hesitating to seek help whenever you may need it.

EXPRESS YOURSELF: Go to *The Understanding Your Suicide Grief Journal* on p. 24.

MISCONCEPTION 10: YOU SHOULD MOVE AWAY FROM SUICIDE GRIEF, NOT TOWARD IT.

Our society often encourages prematurely moving away from grief instead of toward it. The result is that too many mourners either grieve in isolation or attempt to run away from their grief through various means.

During ancient times, stoic philosophers encouraged their followers not to mourn, believing that self-control was the appropriate response to sorrow. Today, well-intentioned but uninformed relatives and friends still carry this long-held tradition. While the outward expression of grief is a requirement for healing, overcoming society's powerful message to repress it can be difficult.

As a counselor, I am often asked, "How long should grief last?" This question directly relates to our culture's impatience with grief and the desire to move people away from the experience of mourning. Shortly after the death, for example, mourners are expected to be "back to normal."

> *"We are healed of a suffering only by experiencing it in the full."*
> Marcel Proust

Mourners who continue to express grief outwardly are often viewed as "weak," "crazy," or "self-pitying." The subtle message is, "Shape up and get on with your life." The reality is disturbing: Far too many people view grief as something to be overcome rather than experienced.

The messages, unfortunately, encourage you to repress your thoughts and feelings about the death. By doing so, you may refuse to cry. And refusing to allow tears, suffering in silence, and "being strong" are often considered admirable behaviors. Many people have internalized society's message that mourning should be done quietly, quickly, and efficiently—particularly when the death results from suicide. Don't let this happen to you.

After the death of someone loved, you also may respond to the question, "How are you?" with the benign response, "I'm fine." When you respond in this way, in essence you are saying to the world, "I'm not mourning." Friends, family, and coworkers may encourage this stance. Why? Because they don't want to talk about death. So if you demonstrate an absence of mourning behavior, it tends to be more socially acceptable.

This collaborative pretense about mourning, however, does not meet your needs in grief. When your grief is ignored or minimized, you will feel further isolated in your journey. Ultimately, you will experience the onset of the "going crazy" syndrome. (See Touchstone Five.) Masking or moving away from your grief creates anxiety, confusion, and depression. If you receive little or no social recognition related to your pain, you will probably begin to fear that your thoughts and feelings are abnormal.

Remember—society will often encourage you to prematurely move away from your suicide grief. You must continually remind yourself that leaning toward, not away from, the pain will facilitate the eventual healing.

EXPRESS YOURSELF: Go to *The Understanding Your Suicide Grief Journal* on p. 25.

MISCONCEPTION 11: TEARS OF GRIEF ARE ONLY A SIGN OF WEAKNESS.

Tears of grief are often associated with personal inadequacy and weakness. The worst thing you can do, however, is to allow this judgment to prevent you from crying. While your tears may result in feelings of helplessness for your friends, family, and caregivers, you must not let others stifle your need to mourn openly.

Sometimes, the people who care about you may, directly or indirectly, try to prevent your tears out of a desire to protect you (and them) from pain. You may hear comments like, "Tears won't bring him back" or "He wouldn't want you to cry." Yet crying is nature's way of releasing internal tension in your body, and it allows you to communicate a need to be comforted.

While data is still limited, research suggests that suppressing tears may actually increase your susceptibility to stress-related disorders. It makes sense. Crying is one of the excretory processes. Perhaps like sweating and exhaling, crying helps remove waste products from the body.

"Let my hidden weeping arise and blossom."
Rainer Maria Rilke

The capacity to express tears appears to allow for genuine healing. In my experience counseling suicide survivors, I have even observed changes in physical expression after crying. Not only do people feel better after they cry, they also seem to look better. Tension and agitation seem to flow out of their bodies.

You must be vigilant about guarding yourself against this misconception. Tears are not a sign of weakness or inadequacy. In fact, your capacity to share tears is an indication of your willingness to do the work of mourning.

"Life is made up of sobs, sniffles, and smiles, with sniffles predominating."
O. Henry

EXPRESS YOURSELF: Go to *The Understanding Your Suicide Grief Journal* on p. 25.

MISCONCEPTION 12: BEING UPSET AND OPENLY MOURNING MEANS YOU ARE BEING WEAK IN YOUR FAITH.

Watch out for those who think that having faith and openly mourning are mutually exclusive. Sometimes people fail to remember those important words of wisdom: "Blessed are those who mourn, for they shall be comforted."

Above all, mourning is a spiritual journey of the heart and soul. If faith or spirituality is a part of your life, express it in ways that seem appropriate to you. If you are mad at God, be mad at God. Actually, being angry at God speaks of having a relationship with God in the first place. I've always said to myself and others, "God has been doing very well for some time now, so I think God can handle my anger." Grief expressed is often grief diminished.

Similarly, if you need a time-out from regular worship, don't shame yourself. Going to exile for a period of time often assists in your healing. If people try to drag you to a place of worship, dig your heels in and tell them you may go, but only when and if you are ready.

When and if you are ready, attending a church, synagogue, or other place of worship, reading scripture, and praying are only a few ways you might want to express your faith. Or, you may be open to less conventional ways, such as meditating or spending time alone

in nature. To explore ways of expressing your spirituality, see my
book *Healing Your Grieving Soul: 100 Spiritual Practices.*

Don't let people take your grief away from you in the name of faith.

EXPRESS YOURSELF: Go to *The Understanding Your Suicide
Grief Journal* on p. 26.

MISCONCEPTION 13: WHEN SOMEONE YOU LOVE COMPLETES SUICIDE, YOU ONLY GRIEVE AND MOURN FOR THE PHYSICAL LOSS OF THE PERSON.

When someone you love completes suicide, you don't just lose
the presence of that person. As a result of the death, you may
lose many other connections to yourself and the world around
you. Sometimes I outline these potential losses, or what we call
"secondary losses," as follows:

Loss of self

• self	("I feel like part of me died when he died.")
• identity	(You may have to rethink your role as husband or wife, mother or father, son or daughter, best friend, etc.)
• self-confidence	(Some grievers experience lowered self-esteem. Naturally, you may have lost one of the people in your life who gave you confidence.)
• health	(Physical symptoms of mourning.)
• personality	("I just don't feel like myself...")

Loss of security

• emotional security	(Emotional source of support is now gone, causing emotional upheaval)
• physical security	(You may not feel as safe living in your home as you did before.)
• fiscal security	(You may have financial concerns or have to learn to manage finances in ways you didn't before.)

• lifestyle	(Your lifestyle has changed and no longer feels safe.)

Loss of meaning

• goals and dreams	(Hopes and dreams for the future can be shattered.)
• faith	(You may question your faith.)
• will/desire to live	(You may have questions related to future meaning in your life. You may ask, "Why go on…?")
• joy	(Life's most precious emotion, happiness, is naturally compromised by the death of someone we love.)

You may also experience *secondary victimization*. This is when, in this time of great loss and vulnerability in your life, someone knowingly or unknowingly victimizes you further by shaming you, accusing you, or otherwise making you feel even worse about the death. For example, someone whose son had taken his own life was told by a friend whose child has also died, "Your child chose to die. Mine didn't." Comments like these are not only hurtful, they may compound your already complicated feelings of grief.

Allowing yourself to acknowledge the many levels of loss the suicide death has brought to your life will help you continue to stay open to your unique grief journey.

EXPRESS YOURSELF: Go to *The Understanding Your Suicide Grief Journal* on p. 27.

MISCONCEPTION 14: YOU SHOULD TRY NOT TO THINK ABOUT THE PERSON WHO COMPLETED SUICIDE ON HOLIDAYS, ANNIVERSARIES, AND BIRTHDAYS.

As with all things in grief, trying not to think about something that your heart and soul are nudging you to think about is a bad idea. On special occasions such as holidays, anniversaries such as wedding dates and the day the person died, and your birthday or the birthday of the person who died, it's natural for your grief to well up inside of you and spill over—even long after the death itself.

It may seem logical that if you can only avoid thinking about the person who died on these special days—maybe you can cram your day so tight that you don't have a second to spare—then you can avoid some heartache. What I would ask you is this: Where does that heartache go if you don't let it out when it naturally arises? It doesn't disappear. It simply bides its time, patiently at first, then urgently, like a caged animal pacing behind bars.

"Sometimes when one person is missing the whole world seems depopulated."
Lamartine

No doubt you have some family and friends who may attempt to perpetuate this misconception. Actually, they are really trying to protect themselves in the name of protecting you.

While you may feel particularly sad and vulnerable during these times, remember—these feelings are honest expressions of the real you. Whatever you do, don't overextend yourself during these times. Don't feel you have to shop, bake, entertain, send cards, etc. if you're not feeling up to it.

Instead of avoiding these days, you may want to commemorate the life of the person who died by doing something he or she would have appreciated. On his birthday, what could you do to honor his special passions? On the anniversary of her death, what could you do to remember her life? You might want to spend these times in the company of people who help you feel safe and cared for.

EXPRESS YOURSELF: Go to *The Understanding Your Suicide Grief Journal* on p. 28.

MISCONCEPTION 15: AFTER SOMEONE YOU LOVE COMPLETES SUICIDE, THE GOAL SHOULD BE TO "GET OVER" YOUR GRIEF AS SOON AS POSSIBLE.

You may already have heard the question, "Are you over it yet?" Or, even worse, be told, "Well, you should be over it by now!"

To think that as a human being you "get over" your grief is ludicrous! You don't get over it, you learn to live with it. You learn to integrate it into your life and into the fabric of your being. We will talk more about this important distinction in Touchstone Nine. For now, suffice it to say that you never "get over" your grief. As you become willing to do the work of your mourning, however, you can and will become reconciled to it. Unfortunately, when the people around you think you have to get over your grief, they set you up to fail. Actually the more you try to get over your suicide grief, the more you sabotage your healing.

EXPRESS YOURSELF: Go to *The Understanding Your Suicide Grief Journal* on p. 30.

MISCONCEPTION 16: NOBODY CAN HELP YOU WITH YOUR GRIEF.

We have all heard people say, "Nobody can help you but yourself." Or you may have been told since childhood, "If you want something done right, do it yourself." Yet, in reality, perhaps the most compassionate thing you can do for yourself at this difficult time is to reach out for help from others.

Think of it this way: Grieving and mourning may be the hardest work you have ever done. And hard work is less burdensome when others lend a hand. Life's greatest challenges —getting through school, raising children, and pursuing a career —are in many ways team efforts. So it should be with mourning.

"There is no path so dark, nor road so steep, nor hill so slippery, that other people have not been there before me and survived. May my dark times teach me to help the people I love on similar journeys."
Maggie Bedrosian

Sharing your pain with others won't make it disappear, but it will, over time, make it more bearable. By definition, mourning (i.e., the outward expression of grief) requires that you get support from sources outside of yourself. Reaching out for help also connects you to other people and strengthens the bonds of love that make life seem worth living again.

EXPRESS YOURSELF: Go to *The Understanding Your Suicide Grief Journal* on p. 31.

MISCONCEPTION 17: WHEN GRIEF AND MOURNING ARE FINALLY RECONCILED, THEY NEVER COME UP AGAIN.

Oh, if only this were so. As your experience has probably already taught you, grief comes in and out like waves from the ocean. Sometimes when you least expect it, a huge wave comes along and pulls your feet right out from under you.

Sometimes heightened periods of sadness overwhelm us when we're in grief—even years after the death. These times can seem to come out of nowhere and can be frightening and painful. Something as simple as a sound, a smell, or a phrase can bring on what I call "griefbursts." My friend Ken loved the Wisconsin Badgers football team. Every time I see something on TV about that team I have a griefburst.

Allow yourself to experience griefbursts without shame or self-judgment, no matter where or when they occur. Sooner or later, one will probably happen when you're surrounded by other people, maybe even strangers. If you would feel more comfortable, retreat to somewhere more private, or go see someone you know who will understand, when these strong feelings surface. (For more on griefbursts, see p. 126.)

You will always, for the rest of your life, feel some grief over this death. It will no longer dominate your life, but it will always be there, in the background, reminding you about the love you had for the person who died.

EXPRESS YOURSELF: Go to *The Understanding Your Suicide Grief Journal* on p. 32.

Keep in mind that the misconceptions about grief and mourning explored in this chapter are certainly not all the misconceptions about suicide grief and mourning. You may know of others.

When surrounded by people who believe these misconceptions, you will probably feel a heightened sense of isolation. If the people who are closest to you are unable to emotionally and spiritually support you without judging you, seek out others who can. Usually, the ability to be supportive without judging is most developed in people who have been on a grief journey themselves and are willing to be with you during this difficult time. When you are surrounded by people who can distinguish the misconceptions of grief from the realities, you can and will experience the healing you deserve.

Now that we've reviewed the common misconceptions of grief, let's wrap up Touchstone Two by listing some of the "conceptions." These are some realities you can hold onto as you journey toward healing.

REALISTIC EXPECTATIONS FOR GRIEVING AND MOURNING

- You will naturally grieve, but you will probably have to make a conscious effort to mourn.

- Your grief and mourning will involve a wide variety of different thoughts and feelings.

- Your grief and mourning will impact you in all five realms of experience: physical; emotional; cognitive; social; and spiritual.

- You need to feel it to heal it.

- Your grief will probably hurt more before it hurts less.

- Your grief will be unpredictable and will not likely progress in an orderly fashion.

- You don't "get over" grief; you learn to live with it.

- You need other people to help you through your grief.

- You will not always feel this bad.

Now that you've considered what might be realistic expectations for you to have about your journey through the wilderness of suicide grief, let's turn to a discussion of what makes your unique grief just that—unique.

Touchstone Three

Explore the Uniqueness of Your Suicide Grief

"The most authentic thing about us is our capacity to create, to overcome, to endure, to transform, to love, and to be greater than our suffering."
Ben Okri

The wilderness of your grief is *your* wilderness. The death of someone from suicide feels unlike any other loss you may have experienced. The traumatic nature of the death may leave you feeling turned inside out and upside down. Your wilderness may be rockier or more level than others. Your path may be revealed in a straight line, or, more likely, it may be full of twists and turns. In the wilderness of your journey, you will experience the topography in your own unique way.

When suicide impacts our lives, we all need to grieve, and, as you learned in Touchstone Two, to *mourn*. But our grief journeys are never exactly the same. Despite what you may hear, you will do the work of mourning in your own unique way. Do not adopt assumptions about how long your grief should last. Just consider taking a "one-day-at-a-time" approach. Doing so allows you to mourn at your own pace. One of my personal affirmations is "No reward for speed!"

This Touchstone invites you to explore some of the unique reasons your grief is what it is—the "whys" of your journey through the wilderness. The whys that follow are not all of the whys in the world, of course, just some of the more common. As you write out your responses in the companion journal, my hope is that you discover an increased understanding of the uniqueness of your grief.

WHY #1: THE CIRCUMSTANCES OF THE SUICIDE

Obviously, the circumstances of suicide impact the terrain of your journey. I have outlined below many specific features surrounding potential aspects of your experience. As you explore these, I encourage you to reflect on those that apply to you.

Nature Of The Death Is Traumatic

A suicide death is often very traumatic. You have come to grief before you were prepared to mourn. By its very nature, your grief is naturally complicated in that the death is premature, usually unexpected, and calamitous. The combination of sudden shock and previously mentioned stigma and taboo (see p. 23) result in a kind of psychic numbing (see p. 73) to your spirit.

Potential "Why?" Questions

The nature of the death can lead to natural "why?" questions. You may instinctively feel the death was preventable and should not have happened. (For more discussion of "whys," see p. 39.)

Potential Self-Blame

As you mourn the death of someone to suicide, you may judge your own actions, attitudes, and any sense of responsibility related to the death. (For more on self-blame and guilt, see p. 91.)

Potential Investigation by Law Enforcement

Often, suicide deaths initially have to be investigated as if
a crime may have taken place. At a time when your heart
is broken, you may have felt you were under suspicion and
experienced being interrogated surrounding the circumstances of
the death.

Potential Focus on the Act Itself

Some people around you may put more focus on the act
of suicide itself than on the importance of supporting you.
Sometimes the first question people ask is, "How did he do it?"

Multiple Losses

You may not only be mourning the death, but also the loss of
support from some insensitive friends and family.

Support May Be Lacking

Some people do not know what to say or do, therefore they
say or do nothing. The result for you is an experience of
abandonment at the very time you need unconditional love.

Potential Relationship Cut-offs

You may find some people who literally go away and let it be
known they have no desire to talk to you or support you in any
way. Again, this creates more hurt on top of your overwhelming
grief.

Potential Discovery of or Witnessing the Suicide

You may have discovered the body of the person you loved or
even witnessed the act of suicide. This may result in you having
additional special needs and may require an experienced trauma
or grief counselor. This is not in any way to imply that something
is wrong with you, but rather that your experience was so horrific
that you may need special help to support you in your grief.

Potential Autopsy

Often, a coroner will request an autopsy as standard procedure. Some people have strong emotional and spiritual reservations surrounding an autopsy being carried out. If this decision is out of your hands, it can become very painful.

Potential Life Insurance Problems

Many life insurance policies contain a suicide clause that prohibits any claims for a suicide for a set period of time (often two years) from the life of the policy. Some families have difficulty collecting on these policies, resulting in additional grief on top of grief. Consult a qualified attorney if this is your circumstance.

Potential Media Coverage

Some print and television media seem to take some perverse joy in covering suicide deaths. This can be an additional source of anguish for suicide survivors. The public realm may have laid claim to this death, but it is still first and foremost your personal loss.

As you can see, the list of potential circumstances surrounding suicide grief are multiple and complex. I imagine there are some additional influences you can think of. Whatever the circumstances, you will be well served to explore them and see how they shape the terrain of your journey.

A SURVIVOR SPEAKS:

"I have experienced other deaths in my life, but never one like this. So many things came together in ways that make this so hard. There seem to be so many things around the circumstance of suicide that make this so overwhelming. It's too much for any one person to cope with."

EXPRESS YOURSELF: Go to *The Understanding Your Suicide Grief Journal* on p. 34.

WHY #2: YOUR RELATIONSHIP WITH THE PERSON WHO COMPLETED SUICIDE

Obviously, the relationship you had with the person who completed suicide will have a major influence on your grief experience. At one end of the spectrum, maybe you were very close and considered yourselves soul mates. Or, maybe you were "best friends" as well as husband or wife. Or, if your child completed suicide, you may be struggling with the loss of all the various aspects of the parent-child relationship. Perhaps your parent completed suicide and you were always "Daddy's little girl."

At the other end of the spectrum, perhaps you had a very difficult relationship with this person. Maybe the person had an alcohol or drug problem or was in and out of trouble with the law. Perhaps you were abused or neglected by this person. Maybe there were some mental health problems that naturally made your relationship complicated. Or, you might have had a very ambivalent relationship that was full of ongoing conflict. In some situations, it is very normal to feel a sense of relief or release (see p. 110) after the death. Sometimes you mourn for what you wish you could have had in your relationship with the person.

Whatever the circumstances, you are the best person to describe and work toward understanding your relationship with the person who died.

A SURVIVOR SPEAKS:

"I had been trying to help my son for years. I always loved him, but he wasn't easy to like. I know I will always have some sadness around what I wish we could have had in our relationship."

EXPRESS YOURSELF: Go to *The Understanding Your Suicide Grief Journal* on p. 34.

WHY #3: THE PEOPLE IN YOUR LIFE

Mourning the death of someone to suicide requires the outside support of other human beings. Because suicide is a topic where many people don't know how to support you, some people in your world will probably pull away. This potential lack of support can be painful and agonizing.

To integrate suicide grief into your life demands an environment of empathy, caring, non-judgment, and gentle encouragement. The good news is that even one compassionate, supportive person can be a real difference-maker for you. Find a trusted family member, friend, fellow survivor, or sensitive counselor to companion you through the terrain of your grief. This person can and will help you survive at a time you are not sure you can.

Yes, I recognize that asking for support can be more challenging than it may sound. Early in grief it is a major accomplishment to get your feet out of bed and take a shower, let alone have the capacity to reach out for help. Yet, you need and deserve unconditional love and support (see Touchstone Eight, p. 179, for more on seeking support).

Sometimes other people will assume you have a support system when you don't. For example, you may have family members and friends who live near you, but you discover they have little, if any, compassion or patience for you and your grief. Sadly, some people (in an effort to protect their own emotions) like to assume you should be "over it" and "put the past in the past." In addition, some people, fearing they will be insensitive, tend to create an environment of mutual pretense. This is where they know it was a suicide death, you know it was a suicide death, yet the unstated rule is: Don't talk about it! When this happens, a vital ingredient to your eventual healing is missing.

At the other end of the spectrum, do look for people who are more willing to patiently help you by listening without criticism or judgment. Those people know you are the expert of your own experience and gently allow you to teach them where you are in the terrain. They know to use your loved one's name and realize you may need to retell your story over and over. They often offer, when you are ready, to locate a support group or a sensitive counselor to help you on your path. In my experience, these people have often been impacted by suicide at some point in their own lives.

Even when you're fortunate enough to have a solid support system in place, do you find that you are willing and able to accept support? If you project a need to "be strong," "carry on" and "keep your chin up," you may end up isolating yourself from the very people who would most like to walk with you in your journey through the wilderness of your grief.

A SURVIVOR SPEAKS:

"Many of my friends think they are helping me by not talking to me about my husband. But I have come to realize I need to talk about him and what happened. People don't think they should use the word suicide, but I need to hear it."

EXPRESS YOURSELF: Go to *The Understanding Your Suicide Grief Journal* on p. 38.

WHY #4: YOUR UNIQUE PERSONALITY

What words would you use to describe yourself? What words would people use to describe you? Are you a serious person? Lighthearted? Quiet and deeply reflective? Are you a nurturer? A fixer? Are you openly expressive or do you tend to naturally inhibit your emotions? In other words, what is your personality like?

The point is that whatever your unique personality, rest assured it will be reflected in your grief. For example, if you are quiet by nature, you may express your grief quietly. If you tend to be expressive, you may openly express how you feel about your grief.

How you have responded to other changes, losses, or crises in your life may be consistent with how you respond to this death. If you tend to run away from stressful aspects of life, you may have an instinct to do the same thing now. If, however, you have always confronted crisis head on and openly, you may walk right into the

---

Personality Types

Your grief will be expressed in your natural style of relating. I have outlined several different personality types below. See if one describes you more than another.

The Thinker: This personality often tries to stay in their head, seeing the world through rational thought. They may see expressing emotions as being "soft" and not serving much purpose.

The Feeler: This personality is highly sensitive and intuitive. Other people might perceive them as "overly-emotional" or "very sensitive."

The Stoic: This personality is the strong and silent type. It may seem like there is a barrier between them and what is going on around them.

---

center of the wilderness. Keep in mind there is no one right and only way to mourn. Part of your experience will be to accept that you are mourning in ways that reflect your unique personality.

A SURVIVOR SPEAKS:

"I have always been a person who thinks better than I feel. Yet, now I realize I have no choice but to stop thinking in my head, and really feel with my heart. It is so scary, but I'm doing the best I can."

EXPRESS YOURSELF: Go to *The Understanding Your Suicide Grief Journal* on p. 41.

WHY #5: THE UNIQUE PERSONALITY OF THE PERSON WHO COMPLETED SUICIDE

Just as your own personality is reflected in your grief journey, so, too, is the unique personality of the person who completed suicide. What was this person like? What did he or she bring to the dance of your life? You, in part, have known who you were based on having this person in your life. Now you have essentially lost a "mirror" that helped you know who you were. The world feels different without him or her in it.

In part, personality is the sum total of all the characteristics that made this person who he or she was. The way she talked, the way he smiled, the way she ate her food, the way he worked, the way she related to the world around her—all these and so many more little things go into creating personality. It's no wonder there's so much to miss and that grief is so naturally complex when all these little things are gone all at once. Also, depending on the relationship you had, there may be things about the person that you *don't* miss.

So ask yourself: What do I miss about this person? What, if anything, do I not miss? Is there anything I wish I could have changed (but realize I couldn't) about his or her personality?

Whatever your feelings are about the personality of the person who completed suicide, find someone who will encourage you to talk about him or her openly and honestly. The key is finding someone you can trust who will listen to you without sitting in judgment of you. Yes, authentic mourning requires you be open about what you miss and what you don't miss about this person's personality. If you don't have someone who can listen to you, at the very least write about it in the accompanying journal.

A SURVIVOR SPEAKS:

"He struggled with depression for years, but when he told a joke, he got this huge smile on his face. Yep, that is what I miss so very much, that big smile that could make me so happy to be around him."

EXPRESS YOURSELF: Go to *The Understanding Your Suicide Grief Journal* on p. 43.

WHY #6: YOUR GENDER

Your gender may not only influence your grief, but also the way others relate to you. While this is not always true, men are often encouraged and expected to "be strong" and restrained. Men tend to grieve more privately, making them at risk for putting their mourning on hold. And when men do mourn, they often do so in the company of fewer people than women do.

I have also observed that women are more likely to seek the support of a counselor or attend a support group. Men often return to work more quickly than women do, seeming to find some support in the structure and demands that are inherent to the tasks at hand.

At bottom, here is an obvious truth: Men and women are different! Based on that reality, we are going to be influenced by our gender when it comes to mourning. This also relates to the "pressure-cooker phenomenon." After a suicide death, everyone in a family has a high need to feel understood and little capacity to be understanding. Combine this with gender differences and you are set up to feel distant from each other. This can be particularly true for any of you as parents who are mourning the suicide death of your precious child.

I cannot emphasize enough that to take pressure off the pressure-cooker, you must, one, be respectful of how you will mourn differently than each other (that doesn't mean you don't love each other) and two, you must seek support outside of each other to release some of the pressure you feel in your relationship. Actually, by seeking outside support, you will ultimately have more to give each other.

Obviously, we must be careful when it comes to generalizations about gender differences. Sometimes too much is made of the difference between gender and not enough is made of the organic capacity to grieve and mourn. Once you welcome mourning into your heart, willingness and capacity to mourn often transcend gender.

A SURVIVOR SPEAKS:

"I was always told that to be a man, you shouldn't cry. But now I have no choice but to cry. If I don't, I will come apart at the seams."

EXPRESS YOURSELF: Go to *The Understanding Your Suicide Grief Journal* on p. 49.

WHY #7: YOUR CULTURAL/ETHNIC/RELIGIOUS/ SPIRITUAL BACKGROUND

Your cultural and ethnic background as well as your personal belief system can have a tremendous impact on your journey into grief. When I say culture, I mean the values, rules (spoken and unspoken), and traditions that guide you and your family. Often these values, rules, and traditions have been handed down generation after generation and are shaped by the countries or areas of the world your family originally came from.

For example, some cultures are more expressive of feelings (Italian, Irish), whereas others may be more stoic (English, German). Again, while we want to avoid the trap of over-generalizing, ask yourself how the culture that has been passed down to you influences your grief.

Your religious or spiritual life might be deepened, challenged, renewed, or changed as part of your grief experience. Suicide grief can naturally disrupt the spiritual terrain of your life, and you may well find yourself questioning your beliefs as part of your work of mourning.

As you are probably aware, suicide has a long and complex history with religion. It wasn't all that long ago that suicide was thought to be a sin by almost all major faiths. Thank God that in contemporary times and surrounded by much information and education, suicide is no longer considered a sin by the majority of world religions. Many, but not all, communities of faith offer compassion and support to survivors. If you are part of a faith community, I certainly hope and pray that is your experience. If not, be assured that there are many faith communities that can and will support you in your grief.

Let me be very direct with you—if you turn to a clergyperson for support and he or she tells you that suicide is an unpardonable sin, go someplace else to get the support and non-judgment you both need and deserve. And remember what someone wise once said, "The God I have come to believe in is not in the judging business." Find someone to support you who is a good fit for your spiritual needs right now. Also, if you are not a person of religion, don't allow people to force you to "find God" or seek out religious answers that do not speak to you. Your journey through the terrain of your healing is yours alone, and the paths you take to do that are up to you.

Yes, when someone you are connected to completes suicide, you may feel very close to God or a Higher Power, or you may feel distant, perhaps even hostile. You may find yourself asking questions such as, "Why has this happened to me?" or "Where is God in this?" When you are faced with a suicide, you are faced with mystery. No, you may not discover answers to your questions about faith or spirituality, but that doesn't mean you should not ask them. After all, the greatest religious figures in history have done this very same thing. As I mentioned earlier in this book, mystery is actually the ancient name for God, and God can handle your questions.

Faith means to believe in something for which there is no proof. For some people, faith means believing in and following a set of religious rules. For others, faith is a belief in God, a spiritual presence, or a force that is greater than we are. Whatever your beliefs, in befriending the mystery surrounding the suicide of someone you love, there is an acknowledgment that certain things cannot be changed. Yet, even as the reality of the death cannot be altered, you and I can have hope for our healing.

I would be remiss if I didn't warn you to be alert to folks who project to you that if you "have faith," you can bypass the need to mourn. If you internalize this misconception, you will set yourself up to grieve internally but not mourn externally. *Having faith does not mean you do not need to mourn. Having faith does mean having the courage to allow yourself to mourn!*

With the death of someone to suicide comes a natural "search for meaning" (see p. 148 for more exploration about this). You have probably found yourself reevaluating your life based on this loss. You will need someone who is willing and able to honor your need to explore your religious or spiritual values, question your attitude toward life, and support you unconditionally as you renew your resources for living. This part of the terrain of your grief takes time, and it may well lead to some changes in your values, beliefs, and lifestyle.

A SURVIVOR SPEAKS:

"I had to change some of what I call my 'faith friends.' Some people have had the nerve to tell me my wife is now in hell. That is not my God. So I have had to be careful whom I spend time with. My best friends are now what I call my 'nonjudgmental friends.'"

EXPRESS YOURSELF: Go to *The Understanding Your Suicide Grief Journal* on p. 50.

WHY #8: OTHER CHANGES, CRISES, OR STRESSES IN YOUR LIFE RIGHT NOW

As noted under Touchstone One, there is often a ripple effect of additional losses that impacts you following a suicide death. Although we think it shouldn't, the world does keep turning after the tragic death of people in our lives. The normal demands of going to work can be overwhelming.

Maybe you or someone in your family has an illness that demands your attention. You may have people who are dependent on you to care for them. You may have a number of commitments yet little time and energy for all the demands you are experiencing.

Whatever your specific situation, I imagine your grief is not the only stress in your life right now. And the more intense and numerous the stresses in your life, the more drained and empty you may feel at times.

You may well feel like your life is in total chaos right now. That is why you will want to pay special attention to the importance of nurturing yourself (see p. 155) and reaching out for and accepting help (see p. 179). Yes you are overwhelmed right now, and it may be difficult to believe you will survive this death. Allow me to gently remind you to be patient and self-nurturing during this time of overwhelming grief in your life.

EXPRESS YOURSELF: Go to *The Understanding Your Suicide Grief Journal* on p. 53.

WHY #9: YOUR EXPERIENCE WITH LOSS AND DEATH IN THE PAST

One way to think about yourself is that you are the sum total of all that you have experienced in your life so far. One "why?" of your response to this death is your past loss history. Perhaps this is your very first experience with death, particularly a sudden, traumatic death. In contrast, some people experience a series of deaths and are overwhelmed by these multiple losses. What about you? Also, what other non-death-related losses have you experienced in the past?

Regardless of your prior loss experiences, there is little that can prepare you for the wilderness you are now in. However, I have found that it is helpful to invite you to reflect on your history of losses and consider how they influence, if at all, your current journey into grief.

A SURVIVOR SPEAKS:

"I have had three deaths in the last sixteen months, this last one being a suicide. I have had to get help because I'm not just mourning one death. I have discovered each death is so unique."

EXPRESS YOURSELF: Go to *The Understanding Your Suicide Grief Journal* on p. 54.

WHY #10: YOUR PHYSICAL HEALTH

How you feel physically has a significant effect on your grief. We know that your immune system is compromised when you experience death loss, particularly a sudden, traumatic death.

Perhaps you have an existing illness that was already impacting your life. If you are physically ill, your body symptoms may actually inhibit some of your capacity to mourn at emotional and spiritual levels. We will discuss this important issue further in the self-care chapter (see p. 157). You might also consider browsing my book entitled *Healing Your Grieving Body: 100 Physical*

Practices for Mourners. For now, please consider that taking care of yourself physically is one of the best things you can do to lay the foundation for your need to mourn well, so you can eventually go on to live well. Yes, despite what you believe right now, you can and will go on to experience the miracle of healing and discover renewed purpose in your life.

EXPRESS YOURSELF: Go to *The Understanding Your Suicide Grief Journal* on p. 55.

FROM MOURNING THE "WHYS" OF YOUR JOURNEY TO THE "WHATS"

What else are you aware of that is shaping your unique grief journey? There are probably other factors, large and small, that are influencing your grief right now. What are they? I invite you to reflect on them and to write about them in your companion journal.

EXPRESS YOURSELF: Go to *The Understanding Your Suicide Grief Journal* on p. 55.

The "whys" of your journey (the unique reasons your grief is what it is) have, I hope and trust, been helpful for you to explore in Touchstone Three. Now we can go on to explore *what* feelings or responses you are having based on these influences. As I noted early on in this resource, a big part of healing from suicide grief is giving expression to (actively mourning) your many thought and feelings. In the next chapter, you and I together will explore various dimensions of your response, and you can learn to gently befriend the ones that apply to your unique experience. Again, thanks for allowing me the honor of companioning you on this difficult but necessary journey. Also, please allow me to remind you to make use of your journal and support group as we continue through the Touchstones.

Touchstone Four

Explore Your Feelings of Loss

A SURVIVOR SPEAKS:

"As hard as it is to do, I have learned I have to feel my grief to heal my grief. Part of me wanted to deny my feelings of loss and try to put this behind me. It simply didn't work. The grief was so powerful and overwhelming that it demanded my attention."

Stepping into the wilderness of your many feelings of grief is an important and sacred part of your life right now. It is my experience that we cannot heal what we cannot feel or do not allow ourselves to feel. Being in the wilderness of your emotions invites you to get to know your authentic self and feel the depth of your response to the death of someone you love as a result of suicide.

Suicide grief creates profound disruption in almost all areas of your life. It challenges all you know about yourself and the world around you. This journey rocks the complete foundation of your entire being. Suicide is synonymous with disruption, chaos, and change—all of which bring a multitude of overwhelming emotions. Taking ownership of your wilderness emotions is the only way to eventually re-orient and survive this life-changing experience. And, as your companion, I urge you to remember: Out of the darkness will eventually come light! Be patient, be steadfast, and be self-compassionate as we explore this important Touchstone.

THE IMPORTANCE OF EXPERIENCING AND EXPRESSING YOUR FEELINGS

As overwhelming as your emotions may seem, they are true expressions of where you are in the terrain of your journey. Rather than deny, inhibit, self-treat, or go around them (all of which can be tempting to want to do), I want to help you recognize and learn from them. Yes, as I noted in Touchstone One, it's actually this process of becoming friendly with your feelings that will help you heal, or become whole again. In some ways I have found it helpful to think of our feelings as our teachers. The healing of the wounds of suicide grief starts with an awareness of our feelings. So, as much as you may want to run from your feelings of profound grief, I gently encourage you to be open to your teachers!

Now, some people say to me, "What is the point of experiencing and expressing feelings if they don't change anything?" I get this question often from people experiencing the grief that comes with suicide.

It's true that experiencing your feelings and talking about your feelings does not change what you are going through. However, self-expression does have the capacity to change you and the way you see the world around you. Putting your feelings into words gives them meaning and shape. *Feelings are certainly not punishments, they are information.* Remember, you have been torn apart. Allow me the privilege of helping you reconstruct yourself.

Authentic mourning creates what is called *perturbation*, which is "the capacity to experience change and movement." The word *feeling* originates from an Indo-European root and literally means "touch." So, it is in expressing your feelings that you activate your capacity to be touched and changed by experiences you encounter along life's path.

Therefore, to be able to integrate the grief that comes with suicide requires that you are touched by what you experience. When you cannot, or choose not to, feel your feelings, you become closed in your ability to use or be changed by them, and instead of experiencing movement, you become STUCK.

Actually, feelings have one ambition in life—to be felt. Emotions want and try to demand attention. However, if you deny, inhibit, or self-treat your feelings, your pain will actually last longer. Honoring feelings is the same as being honest and accepting feelings. *I always remind people I companion in grief that feelings wait on welcome, not on time.*

Catharsis

A Greek word meaning "purging" or "purification." The process of bringing feelings to consciousness.

To express means, in part, to press out, to make known, to reveal. When we have strong feelings and we don't express them, we risk exploding. I don't want you to explode. Expression actually allows you a kind of freedom: the freedom to recognize and integrate your emotions in their fullest form.

Please don't think of your feelings as "negative;" instead, think of them as necessary. If you perceive some of your feelings, such as anger, sadness, and anxiety, as negative, you will not gain anything helpful from them. To ultimately heal, you will be required to drop any conditioning or judgments that your emotions are negative. Being open to the healing you will eventually experience means, in part, being open to any and all of your feelings.

This expression of feelings that brings release from the risk of explosion even has another fancy-sounding term: *catharsis*.

The beauty of this process is that you don't even need to understand what you are feeling in order to express it. You will have time down the line to sort out the texture of your many feelings and explore their origins. For now, let's just create an opportunity for you to befriend whatever thoughts and feelings you are having.

My hope is that this Touchstone will help you see how *natural* your many thoughts, feelings, and behaviors are. I have companioned hundreds of suicide survivors, and they have taught me about this journey. I have also walked this walk myself. One of the most important things I have learned is that the eventual healing that we experience as survivors is *not a task, it is a need.* It simply requires your willingness. Follow your willingness and allow it to bless you, and allow your willingness to bring the miracle of healing to you!

Rest assured that whatever your thoughts and feelings, while in one sense they are completely unique to you, they are also usually a common human response to a suicide death. Questions throughout this section of your companion journal will encourage you to see how a particular feeling I am describing is, or has been, a part of your personal experience. Your journal is one place to describe your experience and familiarize yourself with various dimensions of your unique journey—to tell your story.

As you explore the feelings that relate to your journey, remember that what you are doing is a vital part of your eventual healing. Keep in mind that although you may not have experienced some of the thoughts and feelings described in this chapter, you may in the future. In addition, these dimensions of potential feelings may be part of your experience, but they don't always unfold neatly in an orderly and predictable way.

POTENTIAL DIMENSIONS OF SUICIDE GRIEF:

Shock, Numbness, Denial, Disbelief

Disorganization, Confusion, Searching, Yearning

Anxiety, Fear, Panic

Explosive Emotions

Guilt, Regret, Self-Blame, Shame, Embarrassment

Sadness, Depression, Loneliness, Vulnerability

Relief, Release

Integration, Reconciliation

Now, allow me to help you take a closer look at some of the feelings you might experience in your grief journey:

SHOCK, NUMBNESS, DENIAL, AND DISBELIEF

When you first learn of a suicide death, it is instinctive to need to push away your new reality. By the time you have picked up this book and are reading, your initial shock has likely softened. However, as you look back on some of your initial responses, you will probably be able to relate to many of the following aspects of your experience.

"It feels like a dream," people in early grief from a suicide death often say. "I feel like I might wake up and this will not have happened." Looking back, there is often a total sense of unreality.

Thank goodness for shock, numbness, and disbelief! Other words that survivors use to describe their initial grief are *dazed* and *stunned*. These feelings are nature's way of temporarily protecting you from the full reality of the sudden, tragic death. They help insulate you psychologically until you are more able to tolerate what you don't want to believe. In essence, these feelings serve as a "temporary time out" or a "psychological shock absorber."

Trauma loss from suicide often goes beyond what might be considered "normal" shock. In fact, you may experience what is called "psychic numbing"—the deadening or shutting off of emotions. Your sense that "this isn't happening to me" often continues much longer than with other circumstances of death.

Psychic numbing is like a bandage that your psyche has placed over your wound. The bandage protects the wound until it becomes less open and raw. Only after some necessary time and a scab forms is the bandage removed and the wound openly exposed to the world.

Especially in the beginning of your grief journey, your emotions need time to catch up with what your mind has been told. Even when it is clear that the death was from suicide, you may find yourself needing to deny this fact. In a very real sense, it is a way of holding off the pain and suffering that is coming soon enough.

On one level, you may realize the facts don't lie about the suicide and know the person is dead. But on other, deeper levels, you are not able and willing to truly believe it. This mixture of shock, numbness, and disbelief acts as an anesthetic. The pain exists, but fortunately you may not experience it fully.

You may have found yourself crying uncontrollably, having angry outbursts, repeating the word "why?", or even fainting. These are all normal and necessary responses that can help you survive the trauma. Typically, a physiological component accompanies feelings of shock. Your autonomic nervous system is affected and may cause heart palpitations, queasiness, stomach pain, tightness in the throat, shortness of breath, and dizziness.

Unfortunately, some people may try to squelch these behaviors, believing you should be "in control." They may try to quiet you in an effort to feel more comfortable themselves. Yet, this is a naturally out-of-control, uncomfortable time for you. You have had to come to grief before you were prepared to mourn. Trying to "control" yourself would mean suppressing your intuitive response to this sudden, tragic death. Don't do it. Remember— your needs are the priority right now, not theirs. During this vulnerable time you will do, or did, what you need to do to survive.

As you look back on this time of your journey, you may not remember specific words that were spoken to you. Your mind was blocking; it heard but could not listen. Although you may not remember some, or any, of the words other people were telling you, you may remember who you felt comforted by and who you didn't feel support from. This is a time when non-verbal, compassionate presence is more important than any words that could be spoken.

Denial is often one of the most misunderstood aspects of the grief experience after a suicide death. Temporarily, denial, like shock and psychic numbing, is a great gift. It helps you survive.

However, denial should soften over time as you mourn and as
you acknowledge, slowly and in doses, that the person is really
dead. While denial is helpful—even necessary—early in your
grief, ongoing denial clearly blocks the path to healing. For more
exploration of this critical topic, see p. 28 under Touchstone
One where I outline the important distinctions between shock
and denial. At bottom, if you cannot accept the reality of the
death, you cannot mourn it in ways that allow for the miracle of
healing. So, remember the following, "Blessed are those who
mourn openly and honestly, allowing themselves to eventually
break through the instinct to deny that suicide has touched their
lives."

Often in suicide grief, denial goes on at one level of awareness
while acknowledgment of the reality of the death goes on at
another level. Your mind may approach and retreat from the
reality of the death over and over again as you try to integrate the
death into your life. This back-and-forth process is normal and
necessary. I describe it as "Evade – Encounter." The key is to
not get stuck permanently on evade. Active mourning is a slow
but necessary process of adjusting to a painful loss, and until the
pain can be experienced in doses, mourning cannot unfold.

Remember—even after you have moved beyond the initial
shock, psychic numbing, denial, and disbelief, don't be surprised
if this constellation of experiences resurfaces sometimes.
Birthdays, anniversaries, holidays, and other special occasions
that may only be known to you often create a resurgence of
shock. You may suddenly realize that this person who was so
much a part of your life is no longer there to share these days
with. When this happens, a flood of shock and numbness may be
experienced in a wave-like fashion.

A SURVIVOR SPEAKS:

*" I felt like a robot—detached and alone. I just
kept saying, This cannot be happening, no
way! It was like I was watching myself from the
outside in. Now, I realize my feelings of shock
and numbness helped me survive my early
grief."*

SELF-CARE GUIDELINES

At this point you probably realize that shock and psychic numbing are not something you can prevent yourself from experiencing. Instead, you can be grateful that this shock absorber has been available to you at a time when you have needed it for survival. Actually, without it you could die from a broken heart. So, be compassionate with yourself. Allow for this instinctive form of self-protection. This dimension of grief provides a much-needed, but temporary, means of dosing yourself as a new reality sinks in.

An essential self-care principle during this time is to reach out for support from caring friends, family, fellow survivors, and sensitive caregivers you trust. When you are in shock, your instinctive response is to have other people care for you. Let them. Try to allow yourself to be nurtured even if your instinct is to push people away.

Accepting support does not mean being totally passive and doing nothing for yourself, however. Actually, having someone take over completely is usually not helpful. Given appropriate support and understanding, you will find value in doing some things for yourself. In other words, don't allow anyone to do for you what you want to do for yourself.

You may find that some people feel a need to bring you too quickly to the complete reality of what you are faced with. They may say things like, "You just have to admit it and then go on... put it in the past... other people need you." While I have noted as a theme that your ultimate healing does require acknowledging the reality of the death from suicide, this period of shock and psychic numbing is probably not the time to embrace the full depth of your loss or move forward quickly and efficiently. (Fortunately, the function of shock usually won't allow you to do this even if you thought it wise to do so.) If others insist on taking away your early need to push away some of the full reality of what confronts you, ignore or avoid them. Then, over time and with self-compassion, allow the reality of this suicide death to gently make movement from head awareness to heart awareness.

SAYING ALOUD THE WORD *SUICIDE*

One very helpful way to begin to move from head to heart related to shock is to start incorporating the word *suicide* into the language you use. I realize that acknowledging you are a suicide survivor may take some time, so do be gentle with yourself. However, making actual statements such as "Roger completed suicide," while painful, helps you get it out in the open. You then set the tone for others to talk about it and prevent the tendency to create mutual pretense, which is where you know it was suicide and people around you know it was suicide, but nobody acknowledges that reality. Using the person's name honors that he or she lived and prevents the all-too-common phenomenon of the "family secret." Remember—suicide is death by just another name. Do not internalize the stigma often inspired by a society that often doesn't understand or know how to support you. Yes, use your loved person's name, and use the word suicide. Doing so is a reflection that love doesn't end with death and that you are helping yourself and people around you by acknowledging your reality.

EXPRESS YOURSELF: Go to *The Understanding Your Suicide Grief Journal* on p. 58.

DISORGANIZATION, CONFUSION, SEARCHING, YEARNING

Perhaps the most isolating and frightening part of your grief journey is the sense of disorganization, confusion, searching, and yearning that often comes with the death of someone you love to suicide. These experiences often arise when you begin to confront the reality of the death. As one survivor expressed to me, "I cannot stay focused on anything. My mind jumps from one thought to the next, and I'm lucky to just remember my name."

This dimension of grief may give rise to the "going crazy syndrome." I have had many suicide survivors say, "I think I'm going crazy." That's because in grief, thoughts and behaviors are different from what you normally experience. If you feel disorganized and confused, know that you are not going crazy, you are in the midst of grief and need to mourn.

You may feel a sense of restlessness, agitation, impatience, and ongoing confusion. It's like being in the middle of a wild, rushing river where you can't get a grasp on anything. Or, to use a wilderness metaphor, you are in the middle of a dark forest, and no matter which way you turn, you cannot seem to find your way out.

You may express disorganization and confusion in your inability to complete tasks. You may start to do something but have trouble finishing. You may feel forgetful and think you have totally lost your memory.

Disconnected thoughts may race through your mind, and a multitude of strong emotions may be overwhelming. This is usually accompanied by what is called *anhedonia*—the inability to find joy in things that previously brought you joy.

You may also experience a restless searching for the person who has completed suicide. Yearning and preoccupation with memories can leave you feeling drained. If you discovered the body or witnessed the suicide death, this part of your grief can be naturally complicated. Finding your precious child hanging in a closet, your parent dead from a gunshot wound, or a friend asphyxiated in a garage is a traumatic, beyond-horrible experience. If your mind is impacted by recurring and unwanted images, please seek help immediately from someone trained to assist you. (See information on Post-Traumatic Stress Disorder on the following page.)

During this time you may experience a shift in perception; other people may begin to look like the person in your life who completed suicide. You might be at a shopping mall, look down a hallway, and think you see the person. Or you might see a familiar car drive past you and find yourself wanting to drive

UNDERSTANDING POST-TRAUMATIC STRESS DISORDER

Post-traumatic stress disorder, or PTSD, is a term used to describe the psychological condition that survivors of sudden, violent death sometimes experience. People with PTSD often have nightmares or scary thoughts about the traumatic experience they or their loved one went through. Obviously, the suicide of someone loved is almost always traumatic.

They may experience a chronic feeling of shock or helplessness. They may avoid most people and situations that remind them of the trauma, sometimes becoming housebound. They often feel angry, nervous, afraid, and tense. They are often on the lookout for danger and get very upset when something happens without warning. They usually startle easily, for example, when someone comes to the door or a phone rings. Their anxiety level is continually high.

Suicide grief and PTSD can overlap in some ways with each other. I often refer to suicide grief as naturally complicated grief, and you can probably see how easily PTSD and your journey into grief can interface. If you think you may be suffering from PTSD, talk to you family doctor or a trauma counselor who can help you sort this through and get you the help you deserve. Sometimes, people need help with their PTSD before their authentic mourning can unfold.

If may be helpful for you to know that your response to trauma and to the potential onset of PTSD symptoms has more to do with the intensity and duration of the stressful events in your life than with your personality. Don't think you are "weak" if this traumatic suicide experience and its repercussions have overwhelmed your coping resources. Don't feel ashamed if you need professional help.

Do keep in mind that many suicide survivors are traumatized without having full-blown PTSD. You may have anxiety and anger. You may flow in and out of shock and experience feelings of helplessness. You may feel a need to withdraw at times to restore yourself. You may think about the experience of the death a lot. You are probably in great pain. But if you are still able to function in your daily life and interact lovingly with others, you may not have what gets referred to as PTSD. Still, you may well be naturally traumatized by the suicide and in need of, and deserving of, special care and consideration, both from yourself and from others.

> WARNING: Some traditionally trained mental health counselors who may not have specialized training in trauma grief may be quick to diagnose you with PTSD. So, I simply urge you to check out the qualifications of the person you seek help from and get assurance they have specialized training in trauma grief. I note this because the word "disorder" is frightening to many survivors. By its very nature, suicide grief is complicated and often mimics many of the symptoms of PTSD. It is a real phenomenon, but I don't want you to think you are some kind of "disordered" person. You are a normal person having a normal response to an abnormal, infrequent, traumatic experience in your life.

after the car. Some survivors report things such as thinking they heard the garage door open and the person entering the house as he or she had done so many times before. If experiences similar to these are happening or have happened to you, remember—you are not crazy!

Visual hallucinations occur so frequently that they can't be considered abnormal. I personally prefer the term "mystical experience" to hallucination (see p. 135). As part of your searching and yearning when you're in grief, you may not only experience a sense of the dead person's presence, but you also may have fleeting glimpses of the person across a room. Again, you're not crazy!

You may also dream about the person who died. Dreams can be an unconscious means of searching for this person. Be careful not to over-interpret your dreams. Simply remain open to learning from them. If the dreams are pleasant, embrace them; if they are disturbing or you feel haunted by them, find someone who can support and help you. If you are consistently having nightmares and feel tormented, please see a professional counselor as soon as possible.

Other common experiences during this time include difficulties with eating and sleeping. You may experience a loss of appetite, or you may find yourself overeating. Even when you do eat, you may be unable to taste the food. Having trouble falling asleep, disruption of your sleep during the night, and early morning awakening are also common during this dimension of your grief experience. Many suicide survivors express concern to me that they are not sleeping and eating normally. Actually, I would be shocked if as a survivor of a suicide death you were sleeping and eating as you did prior to this traumatic death. Just as other dimensions of your grief will soften over time, you can look forward to a return to your prior sleeping and eating behaviors. Right now you will be well served to be self-compassionate and patient with yourself.

Another way to understand this dimension is through a discussion of the five domains in which stress impacts your life: physical, emotional, cognitive, social, and spiritual. The stress of being a suicide survivor affects each of these areas of your life:

Physically: your body feels exhausted.

Emotionally: your feelings are intense and overwhelming.

Cognitively: your mind has trouble concentrating and staying focused.

Socially: your relationships require energy that you don't have.

Spiritually: you may question the meaning and purpose of your life.

If you are feeling stressed in all five dimensions (and most survivors do!), it is no wonder you encounter aspects of disorganization and confusion! Fortunately, these five areas and what you can do to help yourself with them are explored in Touchstone Seven, p. 155.

Also, keep in mind that whenever we as human beings experience major life transitions, we encounter disorganization, confusion, and chaos on the pathway to any kind of reorganization. While it may seem strange, it has helped many people I have companioned in the suicide journey to remind themselves that disorganization and confusion are actually steppingstones on the path toward eventual reorganization, healing, and transformation.

A SURVIVOR SPEAKS:

"As I look back, I realize I was so confused I didn't know which way was up. At first I was impatient with myself, but then I learned to slow down and be more gentle with myself. That made all the difference."

SELF-CARE GUIDELINES

If disorganization, confusion, searching, and yearning are, or have been, part of your grief journey, please realize you are not alone. As a matter of fact, as previously noted, I'd be shocked if you didn't have some of these experiences. So, remember—you are not crazy! You *do* have special needs and are mourning a major life change.

The thoughts, feelings, and behaviors of this dimension do not come all at once. They are often experienced in a wave-like fashion. You might have a day or even several days where you feel more focused again, and then your disorganization and confusion return suddenly and without notice. This is natural, so I urge you to not get discouraged.

During these times, you may well need to talk and cry for long periods of time. At other times you may just need to go to exile and spend some time alone.

Try not to interpret what you are thinking and feeling. Just think and feel it. Allowing yourself to let in whatever you are experiencing is actually one of the best ways to remain in an active healing process. Don't get defensive with yourself and shut down. If you want these natural symptoms that reflect your special needs to soften over time, the only cushion for them to fall on is your awareness and expression. Give your disorientation the attention it deserves and demands.

When you feel disoriented, talk to someone who will be supportive and understanding. Sometimes when you talk, you may not think you make much sense. And you may not. But talking it out can still be self-clarifying, even at a subconscious level.

You might ask, as some people I companion do, "What if I don't want to talk about it?" It's okay to respect this feeling for weeks or months (that can help you initially survive), but soon you'll need to start talking about it. Keeping your thoughts and feelings about the death inside you only makes them more powerful. Giving them voice allows you some control over them. Trust that you will "tell your story" when you are ready. The very good news? Over time, your grief story will likely evolve from one dominated by the death itself to one dominated by the living memories of the person who died.

RESTORATIVE RETELLING

Yes, there is actually a term for your need to "tell the story" over and over again. Many, though not all, suicide survivors feel compelled to think and talk about the circumstances of the death itself. This is normal and often necessary. Your mind may return to the moment of the death in an effort to fathom that which is unfathomable. Retelling the story is a natural way of trying to dissipate the psychic energy created by the trauma and trying to integrate the reality of what happened.

As difficult as it may seem to do, create a lifeline to people who are willing to listen to you tell your story, over and over again if necessary, without judgment. Better yet, make use of this book with a group of fellow strugglers who have also experienced the death of someone to suicide.

If you do not participate in a support group experience, I do urge you to locate and make use of at least one person whom you feel understands and will not judge you. That person must be patient and attentive because you may revisit aspects of your experience over and over as you befriend your grief. He or she must be genuinely interested in understanding and supporting you. If someone is not able to give honor and respect to your story, find someone else who better meets your needs.

During this time, discourage yourself from making any critical decisions, such as selling the house, quitting your job, or moving to another location. Because of the judgment-making difficulties that naturally come with this part of the journey, ill-timed, premature decisions might result in more loss on top of loss. Go slowly and be patient with yourself. Sometimes suicide survivors unconsciously try to push away pain and confusion by moving to action too quickly. Remember one of my favorite mantras and repeat it to yourself: "There are no rewards for speed!"

EXPRESS YOURSELF: Go to *The Understanding Your Suicide Grief Journal* on p. 61.

ANXIETY, FEAR, PANIC

Feelings of anxiety, fear, and panic may be part of your grief experience. You may ask yourself, "Am I going to be okay? Will I survive this? Will I be so overwhelmed that I, too, would take my own life? What about other family members? Might they take their own lives? Will my life have any meaning and purpose without this person?" These questions are natural. Your sense of safety and security has been threatened, and you are naturally anxious.

Most important, allow me to address the issue of any fear around your own suicide or that of your family members. You now know the pain and devastation that suicide brings into the lives of survivors. The fact that you are taking time to read this book demonstrates your desire to integrate this loss into your life and go on living. This can outweigh any thoughts you have about ending your own life. If ANY thoughts persist around fear of taking your own life, I plead with you to go see a professional caregiver who can assist you RIGHT NOW!

As your head and heart miss the person who was part of your life, anxiety, fear, and even panic may set in. The onset of these feelings sometimes makes people think they are going crazy. Let me assure you that you are not going crazy; instead, you are a suicide survivor who has been torn apart and has special needs. If you do believe you are "abnormal," your level of anxiety may continue to increase. That is why it is so important to remind yourself that you are having a normal response to an abnormal life experience.

Yes, right now you may feel a sense of vulnerability unlike anything you might have experienced before. You may be frightened by your inability to concentrate. You may be afraid of what your future holds or that other people in your life will go away and leave you. You may be more aware of your own mortality, which

> *"No one ever told me grief felt so much like fear."*
> C.S. Lewis

can be scary. Perhaps you are not only mourning the death, but also confronting the challenges of now trying to single parent children who also have special needs related to the death. For some suicide survivors, financial problems can compound feelings of anxiety.

Your sleep may be affected by fear at this time. Fear of overwhelming, painful thoughts and feelings that can come in dreams or nightmares can naturally cause difficulties with sleeping.

Anxiety, fear, and panic can also be a part of your experience if you discovered the body of your loved one. This is a traumatic and overwhelming experience that impacts your mind, body, and spirit. If you have unwanted and recurring images related to the discovery of your loved one's body, I urge you to get support from a trained professional who can help you.

While unpleasant, anxiety, fear, and yes, even panic, can be natural components of the grief experience. You may worry about small things that never concerned you before. You may fear you will never have control over your life again. Remember—you are responding normally to an experience you never really dreamed you would have to face. The good news is that expressing your fears can help make them more tolerable.

Also, recognizing that they are temporary and will soften over time can and will help you during this vulnerable time in your life.

A SURVIVOR SPEAKS:

"After my son took his own life, I was immobilized by fear. I kept thinking, Who else might do this? My other children, my husband, even me? Thankfully, as I got support and openly mourned, those fears went away over time."

SELF-CARE GUIDELINES

You have probably discovered that you can relate to some aspects of the above discussion surrounding anxiety, fear, and panic. However they personally touch you, please recognize that you will be wise to seek some support from understanding people around you. Not talking about these feelings makes them so much more powerful and destructive.

Also, remember that without some elements of fear as part of your grief, you might not discover you have some courage. In part, courage is that capacity to understand your fears are normal, yet face them anyway—to have faith, if you will! These natural symptoms also alert you to things that need your attention. You might have to make some changes to reduce your stress whenever possible, or if you are having panic attacks that immobilize you, you will probably have to get some outside help.

You want to be certain you do not allow your fears and anxieties to go unexpressed. If you don't talk about them, you may find yourself retreating from other people and from the world in general. Some suicide survivors become prisoners in their own homes. They repress their anxiety, fear, and panic only to discover that these feelings are repressing them. Don't let this happen to you.

Consider using some deep breathing exercises to help you with any anxiety you may be experiencing. Write in the companion journal to help you sort out your thoughts, feelings, and experiences. Journaling, if it is a good match for you, can be a powerful way to help track your progress. It also allows you to get thoughts on paper instead of holding them in your head, where they are more likely to keep getting in the way throughout the day and night. Also, remember that building in a regular exercise program can do wonders to help with anxiety (see p. 157 for more on physical self-care). Of course, one additional possibility is going to see a good counselor (see p. 188 for considerations when selecting a counselor).

EXPRESS YOURSELF: Go to *The Understanding Your Suicide Grief Journal* on p. 64.

EXPLOSIVE EMOTIONS

The sense of overwhelming loss that suicide brings about naturally provides fuel for the potential of various explosive emotions. As you come to acknowledge the reality of this traumatic death, emotions of *protest* often call out for expression. Anger, blame, terror, even rage are explosive emotions that may be part of your experience. Again—these are natural emotions, but some survivors have taught me they find them frightening, particularly when they are focused on the person who has completed suicide.

I have found that it helps to understand that all of these explosive feelings are, fundamentally, a form of protest. We know that it is actually psycho-biologically instinctive in the face of traumatic loss to protest—to dislike your new reality and want to change it in some way.

You may direct your instinctive need to protest toward the person who completed suicide. "How could you abandon me, your family, your friends, and give up on living!" You may be mad at God. You may be mad at friends, family members, investigative officers, or anyone who is available. You may feel a deep, visceral anger inside of you. You may feel raw and exposed. You may even be frightened by the depth of your explosive emotions.

So, explosive emotions can be an instinctive means of protesting a new reality that you don't like. They can help you survive when the world around you doesn't feel safe. It makes good sense that the emotional defense against fear is anger. This entire experience doesn't feel *fair* or *right*. It feels *unfair* and *all wrong!* Anger and these other explosive emotions can help you feel like you have some element of control at a time

Protest is an instinctive attempt to get back what you lost that you value.

when you naturally feel out of control. They also help counter more passive, painful feelings of despair and sadness.

Unfortunately, some people around you may not understand how natural and necessary your explosive emotions can be. No, you don't want to get stuck in them or have them lead to outward or inward destruction, but you are human and capable of explosive emotions.

Sometimes the opposite of protest in the face of loss is over-isolation and withdrawal from the world around you. Of course, if you do that you will be at risk for grieving and not mourning.

Sad to say, some people around you will probably try to convince you that demonstrating any kind of emotional or spiritual protest is wrong. They may prematurely determine that you should just "accept" what has happened and "get on with your life." Yet, as you have come to realize, it is not that easy. When you do show symptoms of protest, there are bound to be some people around you who may perceive you as being "out of control" or "not handling your grief" very well.

When you are protesting, people may get upset out of a sense of helplessness. As already noted, the intensity of your own emotions may upset you (particularly if you grew up in a family where anger was seen as a bad emotion). Still, you must give yourself permission to feel whatever you feel and to express those feelings. Yes, any explosive emotions you may have do need to be expressed in healthy ways. That will not happen if you collaborate with well-intentioned but misinformed people who try to shut you down. If that happens, your body, mind, and spirit will probably be damaged in the process.

Watch out for people who may try to tell you that explosive emotions are not logical. "You being angry isn't going to change anything," they might say. You may be tempted to *think* from a rational perspective that they are right. That's just the problem— thinking is logical; feeling is not. Protest emotions are often an expression from the depth of your soul.

Another problem is that many people oversimplify explosive emotions by talking only about anger. Actually, you may experience a whole range of intense feelings such as those noted above. Underneath these emotions are usually feelings of pain, helplessness, frustration, fear, and hurt. If you discover people who allow you to mourn, you will be able to explore these primary emotions and they will soften. You will experience perturbation! (Go back for a moment and re-read about the concept of perturbation on p. 70.)

If explosive emotions are part of your journey (and they aren't for everyone), be aware that you have two avenues for expression—outward or inward. The outward avenue leads to eventual healing and transformation; the inward does not. Keeping your explosive emotions inside often leads to low self-esteem, depression, anxiety disorders, guilt, physical complaints and sometimes even persistent thoughts of self-destruction. (Please see the important discussion on suicidal thoughts and feelings on p. 105.)

Keeping in mind the important concept of perturbation, you should expect your explosive emotions to lessen in intensity and duration as you mourn. The key is finding others who will help you understand what you are feeling and allow you to befriend your underlying feelings of hurt, pain, and loss.

Remember—you can't go around grief, or over or under it—you must go through it. I hope that as you journey through grief you will be surrounded by people who understand, support, and love you and will help you explore any explosive emotions you might have without judging you or trying to stifle you.

A SURVIVOR SPEAKS:

"I was really beyond mad at him for doing what he did. Sometimes I felt guilty about being angry, but I have learned to accept what I feel as being my real self. It really helped to find a support group where I found out other people have experienced the same thing. Once I learned it was okay to be mad at him, it has changed for me. I think I was protecting myself from my sadness by staying mad."

SELF-CARE GUIDELINES

The place to start is with the realization that it's okay to feel explosive emotions. They are, without doubt, part of being human. You may have grown up, as many did, with the belief that it is not okay to feel angry. Now you have to unlearn and relearn that it is instinctive to protest when loss and death, particularly a traumatic death like suicide, enter your life. (Tip: It's much easier to realize this in your head than it is to actually do it in your daily life.) If you have repressed protest emotions, you don't just flip a switch and start expressing them.

So, my hope is that I have gently reminded you that explosive emotions must be expressed, not repressed, or worse yet, totally denied. Don't prescribe these feelings for yourself, but do be alert for them. You will need a supportive listener who can tolerate, encourage, and validate your explosive emotions without judging, retaliating, or arguing with you. The comforting presence of someone who cares about you will help you seek continued self-understanding of your overwhelming grief.

Be aware, though, of the difference between the right to feel explosive emotions and the right to act out these emotions in harmful ways. It's okay, sometimes even necessary, to feel angry. However, you have to learn as many constructive ways of expressing anger as possible (for example, physical exercise, even humor sometimes). If you hurt others or yourself or destroy property, the people who care about you will need to set limits on your behavior.

A few other key principles to keep in mind:

• Protest emotions are, at times, instinctive responses intended to spur you to constructive action.

• Protest emotions are sometimes a reaction to a sense of injustice, whether real or perceived.

• Protest emotions can often indicate underlying feelings of pain, helplessness, frustration, fear, and hurt. Listen to your protest emotions and consider exploring what may be beneath the surface.

• The integration of protest emotions will eventually allow you to move forward while always remembering your past.

So, keep reminding yourself that explosive emotions are not good or bad, right or wrong. They just are. They are your feelings, and they are symptoms of an injury that needs nurturing, not judging. Paradoxically, the way to diminish explosive emotions is to experience them, even if they seem irrational to you.

EXPRESS YOURSELF: Go to *The Understanding Your Suicide Grief Journal* on p. 66.

GUILT, REGRET, SELF-BLAME, SHAME, EMBARRASSMENT

This constellation of potential feeling *may be* a part of the emotional rollercoaster of your grief experience. Again, allow me to remind you—some of these feelings may apply to you while others may not. Also, a very important warning: Some people will project onto you that you SHOULD feel guilty. I've always found it interesting that we don't automatically *prescribe* guilt in other circumstances of death (cancer, accidents, etc.), yet I often hear people say to survivors of suicide, "I bet you feel guilty." Well, some survivors do and some survivors don't, so we should not make this assumption.

Allow me to be very direct: You are not responsible for anyone's decision to complete suicide. The simple reality is that only one person is responsible for the completion of suicide: the person who did so.

Sadly, our society tends to teach us that suicide is always caused by *problems* and that it is always someone's *fault*. The thought gets projected that the death was not beyond control. And yet, if your experience is anything like my experience with my friend Ken's death, if you could have prevented the death, you would have!

Yes, when someone you care about takes his or her own life, it's natural to think about actions you could or could not have taken to prevent the death. As one observer noted, "Human nature subconsciously resists so strongly the idea that we cannot control all the events of one's life that we would rather fault ourselves for a tragic occurrence than accept our inability to prevent it." In other words, we do not like acknowledging to ourselves that we are only human, so we blame ourselves instead. But of course, *you are not to blame!* Again, *you are not to blame!*

Yes, the tragic, self-inflicted death of someone you care about invites you to explore your "if onlys" and "what ifs." But while potential feelings of guilt, regret, and self-blame are only human (you are trying to go backward and control what you could not control) and some people may inappropriately encourage you to feel guilty, others may try to quickly take any guilt or regret away from you. If you do express guilt or regret, someone might say to you, "There is nothing you could have done about it" (essentially saying, "Don't feel what you are feeling."). In part, whether you actually could have prevented the suicide is not the point. The point is that you are feeling like you could have or should have and you need to express those feelings, however illogical. If you find yourself expressing some "if onlys" and "what ifs," be compassionate with yourself. What a genuine and human response in the face of the self-inflicted death of someone you cared deeply about!

I cannot emphasize enough that it will be vitally important to work through any and all aspects of guilt, regret, and self-blame you might have. Why? Because guilt can become a way of life built upon a belief of your own personal *unworthiness*. Then you risk becoming among the living dead. Because as long as you judge yourself as unworthy, you will never be able to fully integrate this grief into your life and discover renewed meaning and purpose.

As long as you judge yourself as being guilty, you will feel shame. Shame is, in part, feeling sorry for who you are. Shame is a feeling that makes you want to avoid people and withdraw from the world around you. Shame can also make you want to keep the reality of a suicide death a secret. The problem with that is that secrecy feeds shame. After shame comes an unconscious tendency to self-punish.

So, at a time when you most need unconditional love and self-compassion, you may be at risk for administering a course of personal abuse and self-neglect. In refusing to be self-compassionate, you end up punishing yourself, living out your guilt, and creating the self-fulfilling prophecy of "getting what you deserve." Sadly, I have witnessed this unfolding process with way too many suicide survivors, and I don't want you to be one of them.

If you shroud the reality of this suicide death in secrecy, realize that where there is shame, there will be chronic pain. In effect, you will experience as much unhappiness and chronic sadness as you believe you deserve.

By being honest about the suicide and embracing the reality that only one person is responsible for the suicide (the person who did it), the pain you feel can begin to soften. Opening yourself to any of your internalized shame, the pain and sadness you carry begin to melt and you discover you are no longer alone and help is just waiting for you.

Some suicide survivors have taught me that intense feelings of embarrassment are a big part of their journey through grief. Embarrassment, a close cousin to shame, may result from imagined (and sometimes actual) gossip about the suicide among neighbors, faith groups, colleagues, and other social circles. What are others saying, wondering, or surmising about the person who died and the circumstances of the death—and how does that make you feel?

Harbored embarrassment may make you feel that you owe an explanation to the curious who want to know what went wrong. You may fear that stories are being twisted and untruths told.

In truth, much of your embarrassment may be self-imposed. You are not responsible for the choice your loved one made, and the gossip-mongering you suppose may be taking place may not be happening at all. You also do not owe anyone an explanation, but you can set the tone for others by talking as openly and honestly as you can about the death. Just as your grief is natural, so is their curiosity and their concern for you. Keep in mind that they may simply be wondering what happened and how they can help you. Assume the best of others and you just might receive their best back.

The potential shame and embarrassment you are at risk for experiencing is naturally complex. Some of it has to do with how our society has viewed suicide over the years. There is still some legacy from the time when suicide was considered a crime and the person was forbidden a proper burial because taking one's life was considered a sin.

THE DIFFERENCE BETWEEN BLAME AND RESPONSIBILITY

Yes, we loved and continue to love the person who has taken his or her own life. We are hesitant to place *blame* on this person. This begs for a distinction between *blame* and *responsibility*.

Whereas *blame* is anchored in accusation and judgment, *responsibility* is the acknowledgment of fact.

People who complete suicide do not deserve *blame*. However, they alone (even when the decision was complicated by tunnel vision and an inability to see other choices) made a choice. Therefore, the *responsibility* is with them. To hold them responsible does not mean you love them any less.

Despite the good fortune that there has been some movement away from official stigmatizing of suicide death (burial can occur in cemeteries as for everyone else; suicide is no longer considered a sin by mainstream religion), as a survivor you will probably still experience some shame that comes from friends, neighbors, and other segments of society. Sadly, many people continue to make hurtful judgments about those who complete suicide and project that something must be wrong in a family where suicide occurs.

Obviously, it is not only people from the outside who might make these judgments. Sometimes they come from within yourself, making your mourning more complicated. The potential result of external or internal shame is that you may tell yourself, "This is something I'm not going to talk about," which your emotions will translate into, "This is something I have to feel ashamed about." Then, you begin to hide feelings and keep secrets, which never works well. When the reality of suicide becomes unspeakable, your family begins to shut down and feels like a pressure-cooker. The results of hiding, obscuring, or denying the truth are almost always worse than the feared responses when the truth is revealed. In addition, unless you acknowledge the reality openly and honestly, it is easy to feel entirely alone and isolated, as if no one has any idea what you are going through.

Guilt and its associated features can come in many ways, shapes, and forms. Additional aspects of this potential dimension of suicide grief include, but are not limited to, the following:

Relief-Guilt

Difficult for some survivors to express aloud is a felt sense of relief that may occur. This can naturally happen if you had a tumultuous relationship with lots of emotional ups and downs and/or previous suicide attempts. As one father said to me, "At least now I know where he is." Yet, this same father said to me, "How can I feel relief after he is dead?", reflecting this relief-guilt phenomenon. How very human after experiencing the long, slow descent of someone you have loved to feel relieved that this long, winding road has come to an end. If you are feeling guilty about any feelings of relief, I urge you to find an understanding listener who can help you explore this part of your work of mourning.

Magical Thinking and Guilt

"I wish she would do it and get it over with," some loved ones naturally think when they are in relationship with a chronically self-destructive person. Consciously or unconsciously, wishing for the death of someone—and then having that wish come true!—can result in you feeling guilty. This is called "magical thinking" because, of course, your thoughts didn't cause the suicide death to take place.

Sometimes when the relationship has been difficult or constantly challenging, you may have had some direct thoughts about the relationship ending through death. Know that most all relationships have periods in which negative thoughts surface. But your mind does not have the power to inflict death. If you are in any way struggling with these kinds of thoughts, find someone to talk with who will be understanding, empathetic, and nonjudgmental.

Guilt and Anger

Some people have taught me that they experience feelings of guilt for being angry at the person who took his or her own life. "I love him, but I'm mad as hell at him… it is confusing to be mad one minute and guilty the next." Again, this calls out for you to find a trusted person or compassionate counselor to work through the naturalness of this phenomenon.

Guilt and Means of Suicide

This is when you may have done something like lend a gun to a friend for a supposed hunting expedition. Instead of going hunting, he used the gun on himself. Or, some families have always had guns around the house and now they experience guilt around that reality when a loved one completes suicide with one of their own firearms. I have also worked with some physicians who have unwittingly provided medication to someone, not realizing it was going to be used for a suicide. Again, if you are grieving this reality but not mourning it, find someone who can support and counsel you through this.

Parental Guilt

If you are a parent of a child who has completed suicide, you may ask yourself, "Did I do something wrong? … Did I not love them in a way they felt cared for and nurtured? … If only we hadn't divorced maybe it would have made a difference!" These are but a few of the self-recriminations I have had parents express to me or in a support group.

You may need a reminder that you loved your child. You were a good parent. You were not a perfect parent, but no one is. While you have had some influence over your child's life, you do not personally create every aspect of your child's way of being in the world. Our children are shaped and influenced by numerous influences beyond our control as parents. I should also note that in some situations, rationally or irrationally, some grieving parents blame their spouses for some aspect of the suicide. If feelings of blame reside in you, talk compassionately (remembering his or her heart is also broken) to your spouse about them and consider seeing a counselor together.

Spousal Guilt

If you are a surviving spouse, your grief experience may naturally be influenced by the stated or unstated contract you had to "look out for each other." Some of the potential vows we make at the time of marriage can give us a sense that we can always be there for one another. Yet, even the most caring spouse can sometimes feel very helpless in the face of something like a debilitating clinical depression or bipolar disorder. You may also be at risk for believing that others are silently blaming you, and, sad to say, some people around you may actually let it be known they do blame you. Not long before his death, my good friend Ken's lovely wife had decided, for some good reasons, to seek a divorce. Some people around her decided his death was then her fault. Nothing could have been further from the truth, yet some people just have to have a reason and this often means someone to blame! If this fits with any part of your experience, do not try to go it alone. Be self-compassionate and get support. You deserve it!

Child Guilt

I have had the honor of supporting young children, teens, and adult children who are suicide survivors of a parent. While there are unique developmental differences in perceptions surrounding issues of guilt, many of these children have taught me they feel they should have been able to prevent the suicide death of their parents, thus resulting in guilt. Some children feel they must have been unlovable or not good enough if a parent could take his or her own life. Others harbor secret feelings that their occasional, natural feelings of rebellion against their parent—"I hate you! I wish you were dead!"—contributed to the decision to suicide. Adult children may feel guilty if they had little contact with the parent before the death. The parent-child relationship is an extremely powerful one, and when the parent chooses to sever the relationship by suicide, the child may naturally feel many complicated feelings, including guilt. This is just one reason that child survivors of suicide need special, focused care and companionship in the months and years after the suicide death of a parent.

Mental Health Caregiver Guilt

Suicide deaths do take place in the lives of many mental health professionals. Despite one's best efforts to assess for suicide risk and to try to help a client "choose life," it can be devastating when someone you have tried to help completes suicide. Thankfully, the American Association of Suicidology maintains a complete list of resources for counselors who have experienced the death of a client to suicide. Call 1-202-237-2280 or go to the web at www.suicidology.org to access this list.

Joy-Guilt

Like relief-guilt, joy-guilt is about thinking that happy feelings are bad at a time of grief and loss. Experiencing any kind of joy after a suicide death may leave you feeling guilty. One day you will find yourself smiling or laughing at something, only to chastise yourself for having felt happy for even a passing moment.

It's as if your loyalty to the person who took her own life demands that you be sad all the time now that she is gone. That is certainly not true of course. As you do the work of mourning, your natural healing journey will allow you to start experiencing more and more happiness and joy and less and less pain. Perturbation surrounding these emotions is obviously a good thing.

Whatever you do, do not punish yourself for the natural evolution of the fantastic feeling of happiness and joy! If you are feeling guilty about having this kind of experience, find someone to talk to about it.

Longstanding Personality Factors

Some people have felt guilty their entire lives. I hope you are not one of them, but you may be. Why? Because some people learn early in life, typically during childhood, that they are responsible when something sad or hurtful happens. When someone completes suicide, it is one more thing to feel guilty about. If all-encompassing guilt is part of your experience, seek out a professional counselor who can help you work on understanding the nature and extent of your feelings.

Whatever your unique feelings related to any guilt, regret, self-blame, shame, or embarrassment, don't let them go unexpressed. They may be a natural part of your journey, and like all dimensions of grief, they need to be explored. So, don't try to make this journey alone! Find compassionate people who will walk with you and listen to you without judgment.

A SURVIVOR SPEAKS:

"I think I knew he was depressed, but I didn't make him get help. I tried a couple times...but sometimes I say 'if only' to myself. At first I kept these 'if onlys' to myself, but I have discovered since then that I had to get them out. I have found some caring people who really seem to understand my need to review my 'if onlys.'"

SELF-CARE GUIDELINES

If any aspect of guilt, regret, self-blame, shame, or embarrassment is a part of your experience, look for a compassionate, patient, and non-judgmental listener. If you feel it, acknowledge it and express it openly.

Don't allow others to prescribe these feeling to you if they are not part of your journey. Be on the alert for those people who project onto you that you *should* feel guilty. Also, be careful not to assume people are silently blaming you for the death. I have had a number of survivors teach me that they fear that other people will see them as failures because of the suicide. While a few misinformed people might believe or even say this, most people, particularly compassionate people, will not. Sometimes I have found this is a projection from within yourself. So, do not assume that everyone around you perceives you as a failure and believes you should have been able to prevent the suicide.

On the other hand, don't allow others to explain your feelings away. While they may be trying to help you, this attitude will not allow you to talk out what you think and feel on the inside. When you explore any feelings of guilt, regret, or self-blame, you will usually come to understand the limits of any sense of personal responsibility.

As you express yourself, remember—you aren't perfect. No one is. Something tragic happened that you wish had not. Someone you cared deeply about has completed suicide. At times, you will naturally go back and review if you could have said or done anything to change this painful reality. Allow yourself this review time, but as you do so, be compassionate with yourself.

Continue to remind yourself that there are some things in life you cannot change, but that even if you could have done things differently, it may not have necessarily changed the outcome.

One of the worst things you could do is to ignore or repress any of these kinds of feelings you might have. Many physical and emotional problems may result if you try to push these feelings away without giving them the attention they deserve. Remember, as previously noted, secrecy feeds shame. After shame then comes an unconscious tendency to self-punish, and that is often accompanied by retreating from the world around you. I don't want that for you. Instead, I want you to mourn openly and honestly so you can go on to live fully until you die. That is the best legacy you can leave both those who went before you and those who remain after you—to live fully until you die. Again, to do that requires that you mourn fully while you are alive. If any of the feelings I explored with you in this section are trying to get your attention, muster up the courage to go see a caring grief counselor who has the sensitivity to walk with you on this painful journey.

EXPRESS YOURSELF: Go to *The Understanding Your Suicide Grief Journal* on p. 68.

SADNESS, DEPRESSION, LONELINESS, AND VULNERABILITY

Some of the most natural aspects of grief following suicide are sadness, depression, loneliness, and vulnerability. Yes, these are natural, authentic emotions after the sudden death of someone you cared deeply about. Someone precious in your life is now gone. Of course you are sad. Of course you feel deep sorrow. Allowing yourself to feel your sadness is in large part what your journey toward healing is all about. I suggest you say out loud right now, "I have every right to feel sad, depressed, lonely, and vulnerable right now!"

Naturally, you don't like feeling sad, depressed, lonely, or vulnerable. These experiences sap pleasure from your life, yet to experience these emotions is so very human. Experiencing them is not a judgment about your ability to cope. You need not feel ashamed of these feelings if they apply to you. After all, they are encountered by most everyone who is a survivor of someone who has completed suicide.

These emotions are often experienced in a series of rollercoaster cycles, sometimes up, sometimes down. One day may seem survivable and hopeful; the next day you are caught in an overwhelming wave of deep sadness. As life goes forward, you may feel incredibly vulnerable.

Weeks, or often months, will pass before you are fully confronted by the depths of your sorrow. The slow-growing nature of this is good. You could not and should not try to tolerate all of your sadness at once. Your body, mind, and spirit need time to work together to embrace the depth of your loss. Please be patient with yourself.

You also have the right to feel alone in the world despite the fact that you may be surrounded by people who care about you. Hand in hand with feeling alone comes a sense of vulnerability. Vulnerability relates to the attitudes and feelings you have when confronted with the reality of the suicide death. If is often a time of constant ups and downs, a time of a multitude of emotions and disorganized and confused thinking. You may feel uncertain about yourself and your future. You have lost your way in the midst of the wilderness. You feel dazed, unable to focus. You may feel fragile and on edge.

Obviously, I have emphasized throughout this book the theme of being with your feelings as this journey unfolds. If you feel the vulnerability I described above, I ask you not to think of it as "bad" and "avoidable." Traumatic grief brings times of vulnerability. And, at a fundamental level, vulnerability is part of being human. Some things that come along in life are more powerful than we are. They leave us feeling defenseless in ways we may have never imagined. You feel totally naked emotionally, and this feeling is not something you can simply push aside.

This is a time of many changes and instability. You are in what is called "liminal space." *Limina* is the Latin word for threshold, the space betwixt and between. Liminal space is that spiritual place you hate to be, but where the experience of suicide grief often takes you.

Yes, you feel because you are alive and human. Paradoxically, an appropriate way to cope with your vulnerability is to embrace it. In other words, honor this time of extreme tenderness in your life. If it is helpful for you as it once was for me, think of it as a season in your life that will not last forever. Sometimes we want to rush to the next season (often from winter to spring), yet we must still endure the cold and discomfort for a while. You will also find guidelines for helping you with your vulnerability in Touchstone Seven, Nurture Yourself, p. 155 and Touchstone Eight, Reach Out for Help, p. 179.

Now, allow me to return to the exploration of sadness and depression that often accompanies loneliness and newfound vulnerability. You may find that certain times and circumstances bring overwhelming feelings of grief—sometimes something as simple as a sound (a gunshot, a car starting up, a song), a smell (a favorite food, or a perfume or cologne of the person who completed suicide), a sight (a car similar to the one he or she used to drive, watching a lovely sunset), or a touch (a fabric that reminds you of a connection to the person). Some people find that weekends, holidays, family meals, or any kind of anniversary occasion can be hard, as can bedtime, waking up in the middle of the night, and arriving home to an empty house. These natural griefbursts (see p. 51) can bring huge waves, sometimes tidal waves, of sadness. Allow yourself to experience these feelings without shame or self-judgment, no matter where and when they occur. When these waves come, you may find it helpful to reach out to a trusted friend and share the experiences, or feel your feelings and then gently move forward with your day.

Do be on alert for some people around you who might think you should be able to control or subdue your feelings of sadness. Nothing could be further from the truth. Your sadness is a symptom of your wound. Just as physical wounds require attention, so do emotional wounds.

Sometimes your feelings of sadness and sorrow can be overwhelming enough to be classified as clinical depression. After all, the mourning that comes with a death to suicide can share many symptoms with depression, including sleep disturbances, appetite changes, decreased energy, withdrawal, guilt, dependency, lack of concentration, and a sense of loss of control. You may have a hard time functioning at home and at work, which may compound your feelings of isolation, helplessness, and vulnerability.

You are probably aware that your physical body is separate from, but interconnected with, your mind and emotions. Many of the suicide survivors I have had the honor of supporting have reported multiple physical symptoms in the weeks and months following the death. Severe physical symptoms can be brought on by your emotional, spiritual response to the death. It is very real and does not mean you are a hypochondriac! The overwhelming grief that suicide unfolds can result in very intense physical reactions.

The onset of depression can also upset and affect the healthy chemical balance of your body. If you stay in a depressed state for a long period of time without any relief, your body may be depleted of or begin to produce chemicals that can keep you stuck in your depression. When this happens, a cycle has started in which your emotional/spiritual depression now involves the body as well.

Think of it this way: If you are physically ill with the flu, you eventually feel emotionally wiped out, too. Even though things may be fine in your life while you have the flu, staying in bed for a few days can make you feel depressed. So remember, mind and body interact; they influence each other.

If you are feeling totally immobilized by depression, please get some help from a professional grief counselor sensitive to the trauma of suicide grief immediately. As you probably know, help for depression sometimes involves medication, but not always.

Fortunately (though not always), more and more physicians (and your counselor should have an excellent one to consult with) are learning to prescribe anti-depressants more wisely. Specifically, they are learning not to use medications to shut feelings down. Actually, if medications are inappropriately prescribed, this can be another form of defensiveness that gets in the way of the eventual healing process. Medications should not be used to inhibit or suppress natural feelings of grief and loss. That would be a short-term attempted "solution" that eventually leads to more pain, not less. Some people think they need either medication or counseling for depression. However, they are not mutually exclusive. Sometimes both are appropriate but demand a careful assessment by a trained professional. If you're unsure if you're experiencing normal sadness with depressive features or have a full-blown clinical depression, seek out help as soon as possible (see additional information in the section titled "A Special Note About Clinical Depression and Getting Help" on the following page).

Thoughts of suicide may enter your own mind during your grief journey. The suicide of someone in your life has made the very idea of suicide more real to you. However, that certainly does not mean you should do it. You have other choices, like getting help immediately, if you have any concerns about this at all.

Yes, I have had suicide survivors say things to me like, "I wouldn't mind if I didn't wake up tomorrow." Comments like this reflect a need to further explore the depth of your sadness. It's natural to experience these passive and passing suicidal thoughts; however, *it is not natural to want to or make plans to take your own life when someone in your life has completed suicide!*

Again, if you have been thinking of taking your own life, get help right now from a professional caregiver. I also ask you to remember that the very fact that you are reading this book demonstrates that your desire to mourn and to integrate this death into your life far outweighs any desire you might have to end your life. Yes, you have been torn apart and you are in deep pain. But to help your injury heal, you must openly acknowledge what the life and death of the person who has completed suicide has meant to you.

A Special Note About Clinical Depression and Getting Help

For hundreds of years, most people viewed depression as a sign of physical or mental weakness, not as a real health problem. Following years of research, "clinical depression" is now recognized as a true medical disorder exacerbated by psychological and social stress. In fact, at some point in their lives, close to one-fourth of all North Americans will experience at least one episode of clinical depression.

There are a number of influences that can play a role in the development of depression, including genetics, stress (such as the death of someone you love), and change in body and brain function. Many people with clinical depression have abnormally low levels of certain brain chemicals and slowed cellular activity in areas of the brain that control mood, appetite, sleep, and other functions.

In many ways, depression and grief are similar. Common shared symptoms are feelings of sadness, lack of interest in usually pleasurable activities, and problems with eating and sleeping. The central difference is that while grief is a normal, natural, and healthy process, clinical depression is not.

These differences between grief and depression can be measured by how long the feelings last and to what extent your daily activities are impaired. Grief softens over time; clinical depression does not. After the numbing and chaotic early days and weeks of grief, your daily schedule begins to proceed as usual. If you are clinically depressed, you may be unable to function day-to-day.

Depression can complicate grief in two ways. It can create short-term symptoms that are more severe and debilitating than those normally associated with grief. In addition, clinical depression can cause symptoms of grief to persist longer than normal and potentially worsen. If you have concerns about the difference between grief and depression, seek out a trained caregiver who specializes in this area of caregiving.

I have created the table below to help both caregivers and lay people distinguish between grief and clinical depression. I suggest you review this information (placing a checkmark beside those areas that you believe apply to you).

Normal Grief	Clinical Depression
You have normal grief if you...	You may be clinically depressed if you...
__ respond to comfort and support.	__ do not accept support.
__ are often openly angry.	__ are irritable and complain but do not directly express anger.
__ relate your depressed feelings to the loss experience.	__ do not relate your feelings of depression to a particular life event.
__ can still experience moments of enjoyment in life.	__ exhibit an all-pervading sense of doom.
__ exhibit feelings of sadness and emptiness.	__ project a sense of hopelessness and chronic emptiness.
__ may have transient physical complaints.	__ have chronic physical complaints.
__ express guilt over some specific aspect of the loss.	__ have generalized feelings of guilt.
__ feel a temporary loss of self-esteem.	__ feel a deep and ongoing loss of self-esteem.

Here is the great news! Depression is something that help is available for. With appropriate assessment and treatment, approximately eight out of ten people with depression will find relief from their depression. This could include you!

If you even suspect you are clinically depressed, it is critically important that you take steps to get help. Untreated depression can raise your risk for a number of additional health problems. It also may prevent you from moving forward in your journey through grief. You deserve to get help so you can continue to mourn in ways that help you heal. Choose life!

A SURVIVOR SPEAKS:

"I felt so sad, depressed, and alone. But, here is the good news: I reached out and got the help I needed. No one should try to go through the pain of the death of someone to suicide alone. Please get help. I did, and it has been my lifeline."

SELF-CARE GUIDELINES

As you embrace any and all feelings of sadness, depression, loneliness, and vulnerability, you will need the comfort of trusted people—close friends, loving family members, and sometimes compassionate professional helpers. Your feelings of sadness can leave you feeling isolated, alone, and vulnerable. I want you to be on the watch for the symptoms I have outlined related to clinical depression and urge you to immediately seek professional help if you have any concerns at all. Again, depression is something help is available for. *Do not* suffer alone and in silence!

Now, allow me to provide you with some general principles of self-care that can help you learn not to *fight* these kinds of feelings, but to *befriend* them. Paradoxically, the only way to eventually lessen your pain is to move toward it, not away from it. Moving toward your sadness is not always an easy thing to do. Sometimes when you admit to feeling sad and sorrowful, or deeply depressed, people who think they are helping you say things like, "Now, you just need to look at the good in your life," or "You being sad isn't going to do anybody any good," or, worse yet, "You just need to snap out of it!" Comments like this hinder, not help you, on your pathway to integrating the overwhelming loss into your life.

To be able to move toward these feelings requires that you find and make use of compassionate people with whom you can express your authentic feelings. If you are using this book in concert with a support group experience, odds are good that you have found just that!

Talk openly with your fellow strugglers and caring group leaders about where you see yourself surrounding these feelings outlined above. You need people to affirm and support you right now. You need people who will sometimes walk with you—not behind or in front of you, but beside you—on your path through the wilderness.

If talking is an avenue that works for you, keep talking until you have exhausted your capacity to talk. Doing so will help reconnect you to the world outside of yourself. Or, if you can't talk it out, write it out! Paint it out! Sing it out! But get the feelings outside of yourself. And, if fitting with your personality, give yourself permission to cry—as often and as much as you need to. Tears can help cleanse you body, mind, and spirit.

Consider that alone time also has some healing qualities. Choosing to spend some time alone after the death of someone in your life to suicide is an essential self-nurturing practice. It affords you the opportunity to be unaffected by others' wants and needs. Spending time alone allows for reflection, introspection, and development of your inner self. Alone time does not mean you are being selfish. Instead, you will experience rest and renewal in ways you otherwise would not.

Allow me to also remind you that these feelings of sadness, depression, loneliness, and vulnerability do, in fact, have some value in your grief journey. Actually, these feelings are trying to help you slow down while you work to heal the wounds of your grief. It may seem strange, yet depression often slows down your body and prevents major organ systems from being damaged. Depression allows you to turn inward and slow down your spirit, too. It aids in your healing and provides time to slowly begin reordering your life. Then natural feelings can ultimately help you move ahead, to assess old ways of being, and to make plans for the future.

A warning, however: Giving attention to, experiencing, and honoring these feelings of sadness, depression, loneliness, and vulnerability should help them soften over time. Remember that fancy-sounding word *perturbation* I introduced in the beginning of this chapter? I would gently remind you that it means "the capacity to experience change and movement." If you feel *stuck* and have not reached out for help, you can read as many books as you want, but you may not feel like you are experiencing the change and movement you need and deserve. So, don't be your own worst enemy. Care enough about yourself to get the kind of assistance and support that will help you see an eventual softening in your journey. Do your work of mourning, renew your divine spark, live your life deeply and fully, not only healing yourself, but eventually reaching out and re-engaging in the world around you!

EXPRESS YOURSELF: Go to *The Understanding Your Suicide Grief Journal* on p. 72.

RELIEF AND RELEASE

While I defined this potential dimension of response under relief-guilt, p. 95, it deserves some additional attention in its own right. Some suicide survivors have taught me they sometimes feel a sense of relief and release after the death. Perhaps the person had suffered a long, debilitating decline over many years. Some people have been in mourning for a "lost person" long before the date of the death to suicide. Your relief, then, is natural and normal. Understand that your relief does not equate to a lack of concern or love for the person who is no longer here.

When someone completes suicide who in life abused you (physically, sexually, emotionally), you may feel a sense of relief that equates with a feeling of being safe for the first time. This is normal and appropriate. Obviously, this kind of history connected to the relationship calls out to you to go backward and review the history of abuse as part of your eventual healing. Do not try to do this kind of grief work alone, however. This often calls for a caring professional caregiver who knows how to gently support you in your healing process.

Another form of relief sometimes occurs when the person who completed suicide had an extensive history of having threatened or attempted suicide many times before the actual act. Again, while this doesn't mean you don't miss the person and need to mourn, there are a variety of circumstances that might result in some aspects of relief and release for you.

When appropriate, allowing yourself to acknowledge relief as part of your grief experience can be a critical step in your journey through grief. Whatever your feelings, working to embrace them creates the opportunity to find hope in your healing.

A SURVIVOR SPEAKS:

"My relationship with him had more downs than ups. He had some great qualities, but living with him was so draining. I never knew what to expect next. I know it may not sound right, but sometimes I'm just really glad my life is in a much better place than it was before he took his life. Relief—yes, I can relate to that!"

SELF-CARE GUIDELINES

If you feel a sense of relief or release, write about it, or better yet, talk it out. Find someone you trust who will listen to you, really hear you, and in no way sit in judgment of what you are feeling. If you feel guilty about being relieved, talk about it with someone who can help you feel understood and sort out the naturalness of your sense of relief. Remember—relief does not equal a lack of concern or love for the person who is now dead. Whatever you do, don't deny feelings of relief if you have them. They deserve to be honored just like any other of the feelings you have!

EXPRESS YOURSELF: Go to *The Understanding Your Suicide Grief Journal* on p. 77.

A FINAL THOUGHT ABOUT THE FEELINGS YOU MAY EXPERIENCE

As you journey through the wilderness of your suicide grief, over time and with the support of others you will come to experience what I like to describe as "reconciliation." When you come out on the other side of the wilderness and you are able to fully enjoy life and living again, you have achieved reconciliation of your grief. You will learn more about this important concept in Touchstone Nine. But before we get there, let's explore some of the other trail markers to watch for on your path to healing.

Touchstone Five

RECOGNIZE YOU ARE NOT CRAZY

"If you are sure you understand everything that is going on, you are hopelessly confused."
Walter Mondale

In all my years as a grief counselor, the most common question mourners have asked me is, "Am I going crazy?" The second most common question is, "Am I normal?" The journey through grief can be so radically different from our everyday realities that sometimes it feels more like being picked up and dropped onto the surface of the moon than it does a trek through the wilderness. The terrain is so very foreign and disorienting, and our behaviors in that terrain seem so out of whack, that we feel like we're going crazy.

Experiencing something that may seem "crazy" can be a very natural response when coping with the trauma of a death, and particularly with the uniquely devastating trauma of suicide. Because the grief that accompanies a death to suicide can be painful and overwhelming, it can be very scary and leave you questioning your sanity. Many survivors have taught me that they wonder if they are mourning in the "right way" and question if the feelings and experiences they have are normal.

For example, I once counseled a woman whose husband had completed suicide. She came in for counseling and would have the instinct to keep retelling the story of his suicide death. After several meetings she began to think there was something wrong with her because she felt the need to, in her words, "compulsively go over what happened again and again." As compassionately as I could, I helped her come to understand that she was doing exactly what she needed to do. With time and retelling, she became less of a numb witness and began to gently embrace the reality of her husband's death to suicide. Now, years later, she has gone on to help many other survivors understand the need to "retell the story" and realize they are not "crazy." She now realizes that the retelling of the story of the suicide death is fundamental to anyone connected to the person who is now gone. So, in an effort to help, I have created a section in this chapter entitled "Re-thinking and Retelling the Story."

The woman wasn't crazy, and you're not either. You may be experiencing thoughts and feelings that seem crazy because they are so unusual to you, but what is unusual in life is often usual in grief.

This Touchstone helps you be on the lookout for the trail marker that affirms your sanity: Recognize You Are Not Crazy. It's an important trail marker, because if you miss it, your entire journey through the wilderness of your grief may feel like Alice's surreal visit to Wonderland. Actually, your journey may still feel surreal even if you find this trail marker, but at least you'll know in your head that you're not going crazy.

Following are a number of common thoughts and feelings in grief that cause mourners to feel like they're going crazy. They may or may not be part of your personal experience. As I've said, my intent is not to prescribe what should be happening to you. Instead, I encourage you to become familiar with what you *may* encounter while you grieve and do your work of mourning.

SUDDEN CHANGES IN MOOD

The grief that comes with this journey can make you feel like you are surviving fairly well one minute and in the depths of despair the next. Sudden changes in your mood are a difficult, yet natural, part of your experience. You are on an "emotional and spiritual rollercoaster." These mood changes can be small or dramatic. They can be set off by driving past a familiar place, the lyrics of a song, an insensitive comment made by someone, a change in the seasons, a change in the weather, or simply waking up in the morning to a new day without this person in your life.

Mood changes can make you feel like you are going crazy because you may have been told "Time heals all wounds" and believe you should follow a pattern of continued motion forward. In other words, you may expect yourself to keep feeling better and better. In reality, your emotions twist and turn and go up and go down like a mountainous trail. One minute you might be feeling okay, or at least surviving, and the next, deeply depressed and inconsolable.

If you have these sudden changes in mood, don't be hard on yourself. In my experience, more survivors have these mood swings than those who don't. It may be little consolation to know you may be in the majority, but I don't want you thinking something is wrong with you. Be patient with yourself. As you do the work of mourning and receive the support you deserve, the periods of despair and darkness will be interspersed with more periods of lightness and hope.

Hope: An expectation of good that is yet to be.

A SURVIVOR SPEAKS:

"I was okay one moment and then sobbing the next. To say it is like riding a rollercoaster is an understatement. I felt like It was a tsunami!"

EXPRESS YOURSELF: Go to *The Understanding Your Suicide Grief Journal* on p. 82.

MEMORY LAPSES AND TIME DISTORTION

Short-term memory can disappear as you encounter this experience. Entire blocks of time may be blocked from your memory. Long-term memory may still be with you, but short-term memory—such as what you did yesterday or where you just put something—often goes away.

Time may also feel very distorted, meaning that sometimes, time moves quickly; at other times, it crawls. Your sense of past and future may seem to be frozen in place. You may lose track of what day, month, or even year it is. Your memory lapses and your inability to keep time right now aren't crazy. They are so very common in suicide grief. Remember—you have been torn apart and have special needs. Find practical ways to help yourself, such as writing down what you are going to buy when you get to the store. Otherwise, if you are in any way like I was, or hundreds of people I have counseled, you will forget what you went to get!

A SURVIVOR SPEAKS:

"I would have to write a check but I could not recall the date to save myself. I had to try to remember, although I often forgot, to carry a little calendar in my pocket."

EXPRESS YOURSELF: Go to *The Understanding Your Suicide Grief Journal* on p. 82.

POLYPHASIC BEHAVIOR AND THINKING CHALLENGES

This is a fancy-sounding term that means you start doing something and then, right in the middle of it, you forget what you are doing and start doing something else. Many a survivor has shared with me experiences like having started to wash the dishes, then remembering they forgot to finish making the bed, then remembering it was garbage day and they had forgotten to take the garbage out.

These kind of scattered behaviors, where it is difficult to stay "on task," often go hand-in-hand with an inability to stay focused. You may experience the loss of your train of thought for what seems like hours at a time. Again, you will need to be self-compassionate and patient before you see these experiences soften ever so slowly over time.

A SURVIVOR SPEAKS:

"Actually, I felt like I had Alzheimer's. I would start to try to accomplish something and then, right in the middle of what I was doing, I would go blank and just start doing something else."

EXPRESS YOURSELF: Go to *The Understanding Your Suicide Grief Journal* on p. 83.

PSYCHIC NUMBING, DISSOCIATION, DISCONNECTION

As noted in Touchstone Four (and it is so important I review it again here), psychic numbing is like a bandage that your psyche has placed over your wound. The bandage protects the wound until it becomes less raw and open. You may feel like you are present but not accounted for. This has been described to me as "watching myself from the outside in." Remember, temporarily this psychic numbing is a great gift that actually helps you survive. Your emotions are being given the needed time to catch up to what your mind has been told.

Dissociation is a close cousin of psychic numbing. It is where your emotions are split off from your thoughts because they are too overwhelming to encounter. You may feel detached from your feelings, like you are in slow-motion. You may find yourself questioning why the full reality of what happened seems so unreal to you. Again, this is survival-oriented and not only natural but actually helpful to you.

The phenomenon of disconnection is hard to put into words. However, allow me to try. When someone dies from natural causes such as old age, or even in an accident, I have learned it is sometimes easier than with a death from a suicide to retain happy memories. You recognize that if he or she could, the person who died would still want to be here with you. With suicide, on the other hand, your connection to happy memories may be more complicated. Because the person seems to have made a choice that is so painful to you, you may be more at risk for being disconnected from pleasant, even very happy memories. This makes doing the memory work I will describe in the next Touchstone (see p. 144) even more important.

Let me assure you that you can and will be able to restore happy memories of your loved person, but I ask you to go slow and reach out to compassionate people who will support you. Yes, precious memories of good times will return to you because— take heed—"Death ends a life, not a relationship." This potential barrier to recalling happy memories appears to be a natural phenomenon related to the circumstances of the death. Yet, again, allow me to gently remind you, your memories can and will come back and embrace you with love and grace.

A SURVIVOR SPEAKS:

"At first, and for longer than I would have liked, I could not remember any of the times of joy and happiness with Larry. But, slowly those times have come back to me, and I'm so very thankful. Sometimes I feel what I learned to refer to as sappy—sad yet happy at once. And sometimes now I'm totally happy as I recall his smile and how he made me laugh, even when I didn't feel like it."

EXPRESS YOURSELF: Go to *The Understanding Your Suicide Grief Journal* on p. 83.

SELF-FOCUS OR FEELING SELFISH

Especially early in your grief, you may find yourself being less conscious of the needs of others. You may not want to listen to other people's life challenges or problems, feeling like they pale in comparison to what you are faced with. You may not have the energy to attend to the needs of your children or other family members. You may feel angry or disheartened that the world is still turning while your life feels frozen in time.

The reality is that during this experience, you are less tuned into the needs of others and are instead focusing on your own thoughts and feelings. However, this doesn't mean you are crazy or selfish. What it does mean is that you have emotional and spiritual needs that are demanding you give more attention and energy to yourself right now. Your mind and your spirit are directing your attention away from others and onto yourself because you need to do this to integrate your grief into your life. Please do not shame yourself if you feel like this fits with your experiences. Feeling like you are "turned inward" is a necessary part of your grief work. You mourn from the inside to the outside, so this phenomenon is not only necessary, it is natural!

Later on you will be ready to reconnect with others and support them in their life trials. The capacity to eventually give outside of yourself requires that you first and foremost receive right now.

If you need help caring for dependent children or elderly parents, try to find some caring friends and family who can assist you for a while. Of course the needs of other people you care about (like children, spouses, significant others, parents, friends) are very important, but it is okay to acknowledge that this is a time when you are unable to be as available to them as you'd like and need to call in reinforcements.

"Self-pity in its early stages is as snug as a feather mattress. Only when it hardens does it become uncomfortable."
Maya Angelou

Some people may attempt to take your grief away from you by trying to keep you from any self-focus. They may want you to quickly reenter the "regular" world because they don't understand your need for a temporary retreat. If turning inward is part of your experience, be assured you are normal.

When you are in pain after a death to suicide, turning inward and the need for self-focus are analogous to what occurs when you have a physical wound. You cover a physical wound with a bandage for a period of time. Then you expose the wound to the open air, which helps with healing but also risks contamination. The emotional, physical, and spiritual pain that accompanies a suicide death demands the same kind of protection.

The word *temporary* is important here, however. You may move back and forth between needing time alone and needing time with other people. If you stay in a self-focused, inward mode, you may risk developing a pattern of not expressing how your grief is impacting you. As you well know by now, not expressing yourself and exploring how your life is reshaped by this experience will stunt your healing process.

A SURVIVOR SPEAKS:

"I felt so selfish, like I couldn't think of anyone but myself. The support group people really helped me realize I wasn't the only one who felt this way. I have lots of people I love so deeply, yet it took some time and work to re-discover how to express that love to them."

EXPRESS YOURSELF: Go to *The Understanding Your Suicide Grief Journal* on p. 84.

RETHINKING AND RESTORATIVE RETELLING OF THE STORY

While I introduced this important phenomenon in Touchstone Four (see p. 83), it is so vital that I believe we should *retell* a little bit about it again here. As you learned in the last chapter, "Restorative Retelling" isn't a sign that you're going crazy; in fact, it's a sign that you're doing the work of mourning.

Whether you are conscious of it or not, you retell yourself the story and retell others the story in an effort to ultimately help yourself integrate the death into your life. What you have experienced—the death of someone you love to suicide—is so difficult to fathom that your mind compels you to revisit it again and again until you have truly acknowledged and embraced its presence. Telling the story slowly helps bring your head and heart together.

Allow yourself this necessary review. Don't be upset with yourself if you cannot seem to stop repeating your story, whether in your mind or aloud to others. The retelling of your story is an inherent need as you wander through the wilderness. Most people have taught me that it is, in fact, the retelling that in essence helps your journey soften over time. This may seem counter-intuitive, yet I invite you to have the courage to trust this unfolding, deeply spiritual process.

Do watch out for people (both professional caregivers and laypeople) who have not been sensitized to the valuable function of retelling your story. These people may say hurtful things such as, "Obsessing over what happened won't change anything" or "You need to put the past in the past and get on with your life." Or, worse yet, "You need to let go and have closure." Remember—these are misinformed people who have often created defenses that do not allow them to tolerate the pain of your traumatic loss. Blocking your need to retell the story will not help you on your path to healing and transcendence.

Yes, it often hurts to revisit the suicide death. But remember— grief wounds require going backward before you can go forward. Be compassionate with yourself. Surround yourself with people who allow and encourage you to repeat whatever you need to repeat. Support groups are helpful to many people because there is a wisdom and mutual understanding of the need to "retell the story." I strongly believe that when you allow yourself to restory your life, grace happens!

A SURVIVOR SPEAKS:

"For a while I seemed possessed by the need to revisit and retell what happened. As I now look back, I realize this urgent need to revisit what happened was essential to forming a story. I didn't understand it at the time. I just did it... and fortunately after a few missteps

I found the safe people who allowed and encouraged me to do it. For that I say... thank God."

EXPRESS YOURSELF: Go to *The Understanding Your Suicide Grief Journal* on p. 84.

POWERLESSNESS AND HELPLESSNESS

The trauma of suicide grief can at times leave you feeling powerless. You may think or say, "What am I going to do? I feel so completely helpless." While part of you realizes you had no control over what happened, another part might feel a sense of powerlessness at not having been able to prevent it. You would like to have your life back the way it was, but you can't. You may think, hope, wish, and pray the death could be reversed, but feel powerless in the knowledge that it can't.

Also, you may wonder that if somehow you or someone else would have acted differently or been more assertive, you could have prevented the death. Your

"Death puts Life into perspective."

Ralph Waldo Emerson

"if onlys" and "what ifs" are often expressions of wishing you could have been more powerful or in control of something you could not. Lack of control is a difficult reality to accept, yet it is one that, over time and through the work of mourning, you must encounter. These feelings of helplessness and powerlessness in the face of this painful reality are normal and natural.

Almost paradoxically, by acknowledging and allowing for temporary feelings of helplessness, you help yourself. When you try to "stay strong," you often get yourself into trouble. Share your feelings with caring people around you. Remember— shared grief is diminished grief; find someone to talk to who will listen without judging.

A SURVIVOR SPEAKS:

"I felt totally helpless as I came to realize I could not change what I wanted to change. For a while I suffered from the mistaken belief that I could have or should have prevented this from happening."

EXPRESS YOURSELF: Go to *The Understanding Your Suicide Grief Journal* on p. 85.

LOSS OF ENERGY AND THE LETHARGY OF GRIEF

Experiencing trauma grief is physically demanding. Your body responds to the overwhelming stress and lets you know it has special needs. You may well lack energy and feel highly fatigued and weak. You are probably not sleeping very well, and your appetite may be affected with either lack of desire to eat or the tendency to overeat. You may be more susceptible to illness and physical discomforts. I will explore this more with you in Touchstone Seven, but for now, do know that your body has these special needs and will keep asking you to take good care of it. For more help in caring for your body, you might refer to my book titled *Healing Your Grieving Body: 100 Physical Practices For Mourners*.

A SURVIVOR SPEAKS:

"My body just kept talking to me. My biggest symptom was a total lack of energy. Thank goodness that has now changed and I have some energy again."

EXPRESS YOURSELF: Go to *The Understanding Your Suicide Grief Journal* on p. 85.

A FEELING OF "BEFORE" THE SUICIDE AND "AFTER" THE SUICIDE

When someone precious to you takes his or her own life, there is a Before and an After. There is your life Before the suicide, and now there is your life After the suicide. It's as if your internal calendar gets reset to mark the significance of the profound loss.

Some, certainly not all, people I have counseled at my Center for Loss have told me, without much thought or conscious calculation, they know how many years, months, and days it has been since the suicide death. This new way of keeping time is perfectly natural. You are not crazy! Your mind and heart have simply come up with a new system to mark the earth's relentless motion.

I have found that it is normal too for your newfound timekeeping system to come up in some of your interactions with people around you. When, and if, it does for you, realize some people will project they are uncomfortable that you do this. You will discover quickly who understands this "resetting of your clock" and who doesn't!

A SURVIVOR SPEAKS:

"Yes, it is like there was a before and an after. Sometimes I can sense that people wish I didn't think of life that way, but I do and I cannot change that reality."

EXPRESS YOURSELF: Go to *The Understanding Your Suicide Grief Journal* on p. 86.

EXPRESSING FEELINGS MORE OPENLY THAN IN THE PAST

This sudden, tragic death sometimes makes you more aware of how love makes the world go round. Now, you may find yourself not sitting on feelings you do have and being more expressive to people you care deeply about.

Sometimes we love people so much, we forget to tell them "I love you." Or, we (mistakenly) believe that they know they are loved, so we don't need to tell them. After a death to suicide, this changes for many of us.

You may now discover that these three simple yet profound words have deep, spiritual meaning to you. Where in the past you may have hesitated to say these words, they may now come easily from your lips. You may even find that some people don't understand your need to remind them they are loved! But that is okay; you just keep on telling them!

A SURVIVOR SPEAKS:

"I didn't use to say those words 'I love you' much at all. But now I can't keep from saying them to the people who mean so very much to me."

EXPRESS YOURSELF: Go to *The Understanding Your Suicide Grief Journal* on p. 86.

GRIEF AND LOSS OVERLOAD

Unfortunately, some people (maybe you) experience more than one loss in a short period of time. A suicide death may result in a ripple effect of loss (see Misconception 13, p. 47). Or, a suicide may be experienced in close proximity to another death in your life. In addition, other types of losses—job changes, divorce, illness, children leaving home—can sometimes take place on top of the suicide death.

When this happens, you become at risk for grief and loss overload. Your capacity to cope may be stretched beyond its limits. You may well feel overwhelmed, mourning the death of a precious person to suicide one minute and mourning another loss the next. Yes, you may feel like you are "going crazy!"

Rest assured, you're not going crazy. You are, however, in need of special care. You must remember that all this loss is bigger than you are. Reach out to others to help you survive and mourn in doses as you feel you can. In other words, be proactive in getting help for yourself and do not hesitate to see a professional grief counselor. Remember, you have special needs right now and both need and deserve compassionate support and unconditional love.

A SURVIVOR SPEAKS:

"The month after my father's suicide death, my young son was diagnosed with a chronic asthma condition, and then three weeks after that my favorite uncle died from a heart attack. Fortunately, I knew I couldn't survive this alone and sought out the help of a counselor and a support group."

EXPRESS YOURSELF: Go to *The Understanding Your Suicide Grief Journal* on p. 87.

GRIEFBURSTS, PANGS, OR SPASMS

Call them what you like, but this is where you have a sudden, sharp feeling of grief that can result in anxiety, sadness, and pain. Some people call them grief attacks, because they seem to attack you without warning.

You may think that long periods of deep sadness make up the bulk of this journey into grief. Actually, you may more frequently encounter acute and episodic "pangs" or "spasms" of grief that come at you in a wave-like fashion. What creates the "burst" are the events, often tied to sensory modes (seeing something, hearing something, smelling something) that reawaken past experiences. Or sometimes these spasms aren't tied to anything; you just have them come on you, sometimes when least expected.

During a griefburst, you may feel an overwhelming sense of missing aspects of what once was and find yourself openly crying, sometimes sobbing uncontrollably. These griefbursts may make you feel crazy, but rest assured, you are not! If, and more likely when, one strikes you, be compassionate with yourself. You have every right to miss your special person and feel temporary paralysis or loss of control. Whatever you do, don't try to deny a griefburst when it comes on. It is probably more powerful than you are.

I also like to think of griefbursts as evidence that we do not ever forget those who are no longer here. Although the pain of a griefburst can hurt deeply, allow it to wash over you. If you'd feel more comfortable, retreat to a private place where you can wail or scream or do whatever you need to do by yourself. Then, when the time is right for you, *find an understanding friend, counselor, or fellow struggler who will encourage you to share your experience with him or her.*

A SURVIVOR SPEAKS:

"I would be rolling along through my day and then I'd see someone who would drive past in a car just like hers. That is all it would take, and I'd start crying like there was no tomorrow."

EXPRESS YOURSELF: Go to *The Understanding Your Suicide Grief Journal* on p. 87.

CRYING AND SOBBING

If you're crying and sobbing a lot, you may feel like you never will stop, which can trigger your feelings of going crazy. Sobbing is like wailing, and it comes from the inner core of your being. Sobbing is an expression of the deep, strong emotions within you. These emotions need to get out, and sobbing allows for their release.

In many Eastern cultures, sobbing and wailing (sometimes called *keening*) are encouraged and understood as a normal part of grief and mourning life's losses. In our culture, however, sobbing is often considered strange and feels frightening to observers. It is perceived as being "out of control" or "dramatic." (This misconception that many other people have is likely where your feelings of loss of control come from!) The reality is you do *not* have control of this situation, and it is this very loss of control that helps you express your strong feelings. Your feelings are too strong to be "under control" inside you—and their authentic expression can't be under control either.

If you're crying or sobbing a lot, you're not crazy. Cry, wail, and sob as long and as hard and as often as you need to. Don't try to be strong and brave for yourself or anyone else. Tears have a voice of their own. You will be wise to allow yours to speak to you. Let your tears speak, listen to the tears, and heal.

"Weeping is perhaps the most human and universal of relief measures."
Karl Menninger

A SURVIVOR SPEAKS:

"As I look back, I remember just crying like I would never run out of tears. But I always felt better after a good cry. So, I say let the tears flow. You may think they will never stop, but they will...and then they will come again when they need to."

EXPRESS YOURSELF: Go to *The Understanding Your Suicide Grief Journal* on p. 88.

BORROWED TEARS

Here's another kind of crying that can make you feel like you're going crazy—borrowed tears. Borrowed tears are tears that spring up when you are touched by something you see, hear, or smell. During a griefburst, you might be brought to tears by a place or a smell that directly reminds you of the person who took her own life.

Borrowed tears, on the other hand, seem to come out of nowhere and are triggered by something you don't associate with the person you're mourning the loss of and wouldn't normally have been upset by.

Borrowed tears are called what they are called because you seem to be "borrowing" them from someone else's store of pain and memory. They're not yours! You might find yourself crying at a sappy commercial on TV or seeing a little bird out your window. These things never made you sad before. Why are you crying now?

You're crying because your heart and soul are hurting and your emotions are tender. Think of it this way: If you press on your leg gently with your hand, it doesn't hurt. But if you break your leg and then press on it, even the slightest touch can hurt. Your heart is broken now, and anything that touches your heart even slightly may hurt. This is normal and will pass as your heart continues to heal.

A SURVIVOR SPEAKS:

"I was watching a simple movie with a friend, and something one of the characters said about love just touched me in a special place and I started weeping. I guess I needed a good cry. Well, I sure got one!"

EXPRESS YOURSELF: Go to *The Understanding Your Suicide Grief Journal* on p. 88.

LINKING OBJECTS AND MEMORABILIA

Linking objects are items that belonged to the dead person that you now like to have around you. Objects such as clothing, books, knick-knacks, furniture, artwork, and other prized possessions can help you feel physically close to the person you miss so much.

Once when I was counseling a widow, she shared with me that she found it comforting to take one of her husband's shirts to bed with her. She said that as she clutched his shirt close to her, she didn't feel so alone. But as she worked with her grief over time, her need for the shirt dwindled.

> *"Death ends a life, not a relationship."*
> Jack Lemmon

If you like to hold, be near, look at, sleep with, caress, even smell a special belonging of the person who is dead, you're not crazy. You're simply trying to hold on to a tangible, physical connection to the person. The person's body is no longer physically here, but these special items are. Like the woman who slept with her husband's shirt, you'll probably need your linking objects less and less over time, as you integrate the loss into your life. But you may always find these items special and you may always want to keep them.

Don't rush into giving away the belongings of the person who is dead, either. Sometimes people hurry into clearing out all the "stuff" because they think it will help them heal. It doesn't. In fact, getting rid of the belongings because they're too painful to have around is antithetical to the Touchstones described in this book. Opening to the presence of the loss may include embracing the feelings that are stirred up by the belongings of the person who completed suicide. If you get rid of the belongings prematurely, you in effect rid yourself of a natural and necessary medium of healing.

I'd also like to point out the difference between cherishing some belongings and creating a "shrine." Mourners create a shrine when for years (sometimes decades) after the death they keep everything just as it was when the person died. Unlike keeping linking objects, creating a shrine often prevents you from acknowledging the painful new reality that someone you love has died. It's as if you expect the person to return to you at any moment.

When the death is from suicide, I often find that you need to keep belongings close to you longer than many people around you may be comfortable with. Watch out for these people, and don't let them rush you based on their needs instead of yours. You will always want to keep some special connections to this person you have loved and continue to love. If you are concerned about your attachment to belongings that connect you to the dead person, consider exploring this with a compassionate grief counselor. There is nothing wrong with having photos up in your home and displaying some items that reflect your reality that love doesn't end when a death occurs. Go at your own pace and remember—once you have given something away or disposed of it, you often cannot get it back.

A SURVIVOR SPEAKS:

"I have some pictures of my son up in the house and to me that only seems right. I did have one friend ask me if it was a shrine. So, I said, no, it is a temple and just laughed. I know some people think you should get rid of reminders, but I couldn't disagree more. It doesn't mean I'm denying he is dead; it just helps me feel closer to him than I would otherwise."

EXPRESS YOURSELF: Go to *The Understanding Your Suicide Grief Journal* on p. 89.

CARRIED GRIEF FROM PRIOR LOSSES

Some of the pain you might encounter in your grief experience can potentially come from what I call "carried grief" from prior losses. Some people, through no fault of their own, carry longstanding and cumulative grief, often stemming from their childhood.

If this is part of your experience, you are at risk now of additional suffering because of these unacknowledged and unexpressed feelings of loss. You may have many ghosts of grief—that is, many unacknowledged losses—or you may find that your ghost is identifiably singular—a specific loss that devastated you, even if you didn't realize it at the time.

Now, as you experience this death and the need to mourn, you may have some symptoms

Catch-up Mourning

If you are carrying grief from prior losses, which will only compound your current grief, you must embark on a journey of catch-up mourning. Catch-up mourning is going backward and giving attention to any unmourned, unexplored grief you have carried forward from past losses in your life. The purpose of going back and doing your grief work is anchored in eventually freeing you to go forward with newfound meaning and purpose in your life, living, and loving.

(such as generalized anxiety, panic attacks, depression) that are invitations to go backward and give attention to your prior losses that were never fully mourned and integrated into your life. Sometimes you cannot mourn current losses and life transitions until you go backward and work on your previous carried griefs.

Experience has taught me that some people feel crazy because of this phenomenon of carried grief. The good news is that if this does apply to you, there are ways of getting help to do catch-up mourning. If you want to learn more about this and make a plan to help yourself, see my book *Living in the Shadow of the Ghosts of Grief: Step Into the Light.*

A SURVIVOR SPEAKS:

"I had experienced the sudden death of my mother when I was eight years old. After my husband took his own life, it brought it all up for me. No one had ever really helped me mourn the death of my mother. Now, I was confronted with the need to mourn her and my husband."

EXPRESS YOURSELF: Go to *The Understanding Your Suicide Grief Journal* on p. 89.

SUICIDAL THOUGHTS

We touched on suicidal thoughts in Touchstone Four, but this subject is important enough to reemphasize here. Thoughts that come and go about questioning if you want to go on living can be a normal part of your grief and mourning. You might say or think, "It'd be so much easier not to be here" or "I'm not sure I'd mind it if I didn't wake up tomorrow." Usually these thoughts are not so much an active wish to kill yourself as they are a wish to avoid or ease your pain.

To have these thoughts is normal and not crazy; however, to make plans and take action to end your life is extremely concerning and not a normal response to this tragic death. Sometimes your body, mind, and spirit can hurt so much that you wonder if you will ever feel alive again. Just remember that in doing the hard work of mourning, you can and will find continued meaning in life. Let yourself be helped as you discover hope for your healing.

If thoughts of suicide take on planning and structure, make certain that you get help immediately. Sometimes tunnel vision can prevent you from seeing choices. You have the capacity to mourn this death and go on to rediscover a life filled with meaning and purpose. Also keep a close watch on other close friends and family members grieving this death. They are also at risk for suicidal thoughts and actions. If you notice any signs that might indicate suicidal plans, get professional help immediately.

A SURVIVOR SPEAKS:

"Early on I thought I should just join her and take my own life. But then I thought that wouldn't be of any help to anyone, including myself. I found a terrific counselor who helped me through this. If you have any thoughts like this, get help ASAP. I did and it made a huge difference for me."

EXPRESS YOURSELF: Go to *The Understanding Your Suicide Grief Journal* on p. 90.

DREAMS OR NIGHTMARES

Sometimes dreaming a lot about the person who died may contribute to your feelings of "going crazy." Mourners sometimes tell me that they can't stop thinking about the death—even in their sleep!

Keep in mind that dreams are one of the ways the work of mourning takes place. A dream may reflect a searching for the person who has died, for example. You may dream that you are with the person in a crowded place and lose him and cannot find him. Dreams also provide opportunities—to feel close to the person who died, to embrace the reality of the death, to gently confront the depth of the loss, to renew memories, or to develop a new self-identity. Dreams also may help you search for meaning in life and death or explore unfinished business. Finally, dreams can show you hope for the future.

The content of your dreams often reflects changes in your grief journey. You may have one kind of dream early in your grief and another later on. So if dreams are part of your trek through the wilderness, make use of them to better understand where you have been, where you are, and where you are going. Also, find a skilled listener who won't interpret your dreams for you, but who will listen to you.

It is one thing to dream, it is another to experience nightmares that frighten and disturb you. Nightmares can make you feel crazy, and if

"The dream reveals itself in its own timetable, but it does reveal itself."
Thomas Moore

they are part of your experience, I urge you to see a professional caregiver who can help you sort out what is going on.

Remember—a good counselor can be a companion, a guide into and through your journey. Don't suffer through nightmares alone or in isolation—get help now!

A SURVIVOR SPEAKS:

"I found that my nightmare reflected the trauma I had experienced. Some members of my support groups had comforting dreams, but I had nightmares that intruded into my entire being. I got help sorting out what was going on, and that helped me in so many ways. Eventually my nightmares stopped and a few comforting dreams came along. I liked the dreams, but I couldn't tolerate the nightmares!"

EXPRESS YOURSELF: Go to *The Understanding Your Suicide Grief Journal* on p. 90.

MYSTICAL EXPERIENCES

Many people I have companioned in the grief journey have taught me they have had experiences that are not always rationally explainable. Let me assure you that if this applies to you, it does not mean you are crazy! However, do be aware that depending on who you share these experiences with, they may question your sanity. But I like to think that if you have mystical experiences, you're simply mystically sensitive—and blessed!

The primary form of mystical experience that mourners who have experienced a suicide death have shared with me involves some sense of communication to or from the dead person. I have listened to and learned from hundreds of people who have seen, heard, and felt the presence of someone who has died. The bulk of people find these experiences comforting, but some people are upset by them. I have had enough people teach me about these experiences to know you're not crazy if you have them. Just have some discernment with whom you share them. You don't need judgment; you need someone to honor and bear witness to your experience. If you do have any of these mystical experiences, I hope they do bring you comfort and hope.

A SURVIVOR SPEAKS:

"I was sitting in my living room when I had this very strong sense of his presence. It was like he was right there, wanting to wrap his arms around me but didn't know if it would scare me. So, I said aloud, go ahead and hug me... and he did... then he slipped away. It was like he was just letting me know he was okay. I have learned I have to watch who I tell about this."

EXPRESS YOURSELF: Go to *The Understanding Your Suicide Grief Journal* on p. 91.

ANNIVERSARY AND HOLIDAY GRIEF OCCASIONS

Naturally, anniversary and holiday occasions can bring about pangs of grief. Birthdays, wedding dates, holidays such as Easter, Thanksgiving, Hanukkah, and Christmas, and other special occasions create a heightened sense of loss. At these times, you may likely experience griefbursts.

Your pangs of grief also may occur in circumstances that bring up reminders of the painful absence of someone in your life. For many families, certain days have special meaning (for example, the first snowfall, an annual Fourth of July party, or any time when activities were shared as a couple or a family), and the person who died is more deeply missed at those times.

Of course, on these special occasions you may not only miss the person who died, you may also be mourning the loss of hopes and dreams for the future. If your unmarried child completes suicide, for example, special occasions such as weddings or christenings will likely stir up regrets that you and your family will never experience the joy of these occasions in the life of your child.

If you're having a really tough time on special days, you're not crazy. Perhaps the most important thing to remember is that your feelings are natural. And sometimes the anticipation of an anniversary or holiday turns out to be worse than the day itself.

Interestingly, sometimes your internal clock will alert you to an anniversary date you may not consciously be aware of. If you notice you are feeling down or experiencing pangs of grief, you may be having an anniversary response. Take a look at the calendar and consider if this particular day has meant anything to you in years past.

Plan ahead when you know some naturally painful times are coming. Unfortunately, some grieving people will not mention anniversaries, holidays, or special occasions to anyone. So they suffer in silence, and their feelings of isolation increase. Don't let this happen to you. Recognize you will need support, and map out how to get it!

A SURVIVOR SPEAKS:

"Thanksgiving was always Dad's favorite gathering time. Now, every year as it approaches I have learned to take very special care of myself. I survive it, but I think it will always be greeted with some sadness."

EXPRESS YOURSELF: Go to *The Understanding Your Suicide Grief Journal* on p. 91.

RITUAL-STIMULATED REACTIONS, SEASONAL REACTIONS, MUSIC-STIMULATED REACTIONS, AND AGE-CORRESPONDENCE REACTIONS

Similar to griefbursts in nature, certain experiences you encounter might re-stimulate feelings surrounding your loss. Four such forms are briefly outlined below.

RITUAL-STIMULATED REACTIONS are things like gathering for family dinners or a Sunday brunch. You may have been used to this being a special time with your precious person and naturally feel his or her absence.

SEASONAL REACTIONS relate to how the change of seasons can stimulate grief or invite you to slow down and continue to honor your ongoing need to mourn. Be gentle with yourself as the seasons change and nurture yourself if you know you are more prone to being depressed at a particular time of year.

MUSIC-STIMULATED GRIEF relates to how music can activate your right brain, creating associations and deep, often profound feelings stimulated by a specific song or piece of music.

AGE-CORRESPONDENCE REACTIONS can take place, for example, when you reach the age of the person who took his or her own life. So, if your parent died at age 62, when you reach that age you may naturally experience a renewed sense of loss.

A SURVIVOR SPEAKS:

"I was just driving along and a Beatles song titled 'In My Life' came on, and I just burst out in tears and had to pull to the side of the road. I have learned that happens to me and to be kind to myself when it does."

EXPRESS YOURSELF: Go to *The Understanding Your Suicide Grief Journal* on p. 92.

YOU'RE NOT CRAZY, YOU'RE GRIEVING AND MOURNING

Never forget that your journey through the wilderness of your grief may bring you through all kinds of strange and unfamiliar terrain. As I said at the beginning of this chapter, your experiences may seem so alien that you feel more like you're on the moon! When it seems like you're going crazy, remind yourself to look for the trail marker that assures you you're not going crazy, you're grieving and mourning. Can you think of any other experiences you had that might fit in this chapter? If so, drop me an email at drwolfelt@centerforloss.com so I can include them in any future editions of this resource. And just think, you will be helping other fellow mourners when you do this! Now, let's turn to learning about six important needs of mourning.

Touchstone Six

UNDERSTANDING THE SIX NEEDS OF MOURNING

"Mourning is a series of spiritual awakenings borne out of the willingness to experience an authentic encounter with the pain surrounding the loss."
Alan D. Wolfelt

If you are looking for a detailed map for your journey through suicide grief, none exists. *Your* wilderness is an undiscovered wilderness and you its first explorer.

But those of us who have experienced a death of someone to suicide have found that our paths have many similarities. A number of authors have proposed models of grief that refer to "stages." As we agreed in Touchstone Two about grief misconceptions, we do not go through orderly, predictable stages of grief, with clear-cut beginnings and endings.

However, when we are mourning a death to suicide, we do have some similar needs. Instead of referring to stages of grief, I say that we as mourners have six central needs. Remember I said in the Introduction that as we journey through grief, we need to follow the trail markers, or the Touchstones, if we are to find our way out of the wilderness? The trail marker we will discuss in this chapter explores the six central needs of mourning. You might think of Touchstone Six as its own little grouping of trail markers.

You will find that several of the six needs of mourning reiterate and reinforce concepts found in other chapters of this book. I hope this reinforcement helps you embrace how very important these fundamental concepts are.

Throughout this chapter, you will also find a number of grief meditation passages that, when read slowly and thoughtfully, help you work on the corresponding need. These "reflections" are from my book *The Journey Through Grief: Reflections on Healing*. Many mourners have found this to be a healing, meditative text to read at bedtime or early morning time. I hope these excerpts will help you befriend the six needs of mourning.

Unlike the stages of grief you might have heard about, *the six needs of mourning are not orderly or predictable*. You will probably jump around in random fashion while working on them. You will address each need when you are ready to do so. Sometimes you will be working on more than one need at a time. Your awareness of these needs, however, will give you a participative, action-oriented approach to healing in grief as opposed to a perception of grief as something you passively experience.

THE SIX NEEDS OF MOURNING

- Accept the reality of the death.
- Let yourself feel the pain of the loss.
- Remember the person who died.
- Develop a new self-identity.
- Search for meaning.
- Let others help you—now and always.

MOURNING NEED 1: ACCEPT THE REALITY OF THE DEATH

You can know something in your head but not in your heart. This is what often happens when someone you love takes his or her own life. This first need of mourning, a close cousin to Touchstone One (open to the presence of your loss), involves gently confronting the reality that someone you care about will never physically come back into your life again.

Because the nature of a suicide death is sudden, and naturally traumatic, acknowledging the full reality usually doesn't happen in days, but in weeks or even months. To survive you will probably naturally need to push away the reality of the death at times. But as I have tried to gently convey throughout this book, embracing this kind of painful reality should never be quick, easy, or efficient. You may find it helpful to consider re-reading the section in Touchstone Three, pages 54-56, where I outlined the circumstances that often accompany suicide. This can help you see how your unique circumstances have a natural influence on this need to acknowledge the reality of the death.

> It's as if the realness of what has happened waits around the corner. I don't want to make the turn, yet I know I must. Slowly, I gather the courage to approach.

You may move back and forth between protesting and encountering the reality of the death. You may discover yourself replaying events surrounding the death and confronting memories, both good and bad. This replay is a vital part of this need of mourning. It's as if each time you talk it out, the event is a little more real.

One moment the reality of the loss may be tolerable; another moment it may be unbearable. Be patient with this need. At times, you may feel like running away and hiding. At other

> To live into the future depends on my response to the reality of what I am experiencing. Temporarily, I need to create insulation from the full force of what I am coming to know. If I felt it all at once, I might die. But feel it I must.

times, you may hope you will awaken from what seems like a bad dream. As you express what you think and feel outside of yourself, you will be working on this important need.

Remember—this first need of mourning, like the other five that follow, may intermittently require your attention for months. Be patient and compassionate with yourself as you work on each of them.

A SURVIVOR SPEAKS:

"I kept fading in and out from the reality of what happened. At times I just kept thinking it was a bad dream. But it wasn't, and slowly I allowed myself to realize it really happened."

EXPRESS YOURSELF: Go to *The Understanding Your Suicide Grief Journal* on p. 94.

MOURNING NEED 2: LET YOURSELF FEEL THE PAIN OF THE LOSS

Like Touchstone One (open to the presence of your loss), this need of mourning requires us to embrace the pain of our loss—something we naturally don't want to do. It is easier to avoid, repress, or deny the pain of grief than it is to confront it, yet it is in confronting our pain that we learn to reconcile ourselves to it.

I may try to protect myself from my sadness by not talking about my loss. I may even secretly hope that the person who died will come back if I don't talk about it. Yet, as difficult as it is, I must feel it to heal it.

You will probably discover that you need to dose yourself in embracing your pain. In other words, you cannot (nor should you try to) overload yourself with the hurt all at one time. Sometimes you may need to distract yourself from the pain of the death, while at other times you will need to create a safe place to move toward it.

Feeling your pain can sometimes zap you of your energy. When your energy is low, you may be tempted to suppress your grief or even run from it. If you start running and keep running, you may never heal. Dose your pain: yes! Deny your pain: no!

Unfortunately, as I have said, our culture tends to encourage the denial of pain. We misunderstand the role of suffering. If you openly express your feelings of grief, misinformed friends may advise you to "carry on" or "keep your chin up." If, on the other hand, you remain "strong" and "in control," you may be congratulated for "doing well" with your grief. Actually, doing well with your grief means becoming well acquainted with your pain. Don't let others deny you this critical mourning need.

If you are a man, be aware that this need may be particularly difficult to meet. You may be conditioned to deny pain and encouraged to keep your feelings inside. You may expect yourself to "be strong" and "in control." Yet, despite your efforts at self-control, you may now be experiencing a variety

> The grief within me has its own heartbeat. It has its own life, its own song. Part of me wants to resist the rhythms of my grief. Yet, as I surrender to the song, I learn to listen deep within myself.

of feelings at an intensity level you never thought possible. To slow down, turn inward, and embrace hurt may be foreign to you. I hope you have caring friends who will be understanding, patient, and tolerant with you.

As you encounter your pain, you will also need to nurture yourself physically, emotionally, cognitively, socially, and spiritually. Eat well, rest often, and exercise regularly. Find others with whom you can share your painful thoughts and feelings; friends who listen without judging are your most important helpers as you work on his mourning need. Give yourself permission to question your faith. It's okay to be angry with your God and to struggle with meaning of life issues at this time.

Never forget that suicide grief is usually a slow, arduous experience. Your pain will probably ebb and flow for months, even years; embracing it when it washes over you will require patience, support, and strength.

A SURVIVOR SPEAKS:

"I like the idea of dosing my pain from this excruciating loss. If I tried to do this quickly, I would find it impossible. Dr. Wolfelt helped me remember: Go slowly! There are no rewards for speed!"

EXPRESS YOURSELF: Go to *The Understanding Your Suicide Grief Journal* on p. 95.

MOURNING NEED 3: REMEMBER THE PERSON WHO DIED

Do you have any kind of relationship with people after they die? Of course. You have a relationship of memory. Precious memories, dreams reflecting the significance of the relationship, and objects that link you to the person who died (such as photos, souvenirs, clothing, etc.) are examples of some of the things that give testimony to a different form of a continued relationship. This need of mourning involves allowing and encouraging yourself to pursue this relationship.

The process of beginning to embrace your memories often begins with the funeral. The ritual offers you an opportunity to remember the person who

The essence of finding meaning in the future is not to forget my past, as I have been told, but instead to embrace my past. For it is in listening to the music of the past that I can sing in the present and dance into the future.

died and helps to affirm the value of the life that was lived. The memories you embrace during the time of the funeral set the tone for the changed nature of the relationship. Even later on, meaningful rituals encourage the expression of cherished memories and allow for both tears and laughter in the company of others who loved the person who died by suicide.

Embracing your memories can be a very slow and, at times, painful process that occurs in small steps. Remember—don't try to do all your work of mourning at once. Go slowly and be patient with yourself. Remember as I noted on p. 118 that this memory work is often naturally complicated when it follows a death to suicide. But you can and will be able to do it at your own pace and in your own time.

Some people may try to take your memories away. Trying to be helpful, they encourage you to take down all photos of the person who died. They tell you to keep busy or even to move out of your house. You, too, may think avoiding memories would be better for you. And why not? You are living in a culture that teaches you that to move away from—instead of toward—your grief is best.

Following are a few examples of things you can do to keep memories alive while embracing the reality that the person has died:

- Talking out or writing out favorite memories.

- Giving yourself permission to keep some special keepsakes or "linking objects" (see p. 129).

- Displaying photos of the person who is now dead.

- Visiting places of special significance that stimulate memories of times shared together.

- Reviewing photo albums at special times such as holidays, birthdays, and anniversaries.

Perhaps one of the best ways to embrace memories is through creating a "memory book" that contains special photographs you have selected and perhaps other memorabilia such as ticket stubs, menus, etc. Organize these items, place them in an album, and write out the memories reflected in

I can release the pain that touches my memories, but only if I remember them. I can release my grief, but only if I express it. Memories and grief must have a heart to hold them.

the photos. This book can then become a valued collection of memories that you can review whenever you want.

I also need to mention here the reality that memories are not always pleasant. If this applies to you, addressing this need of mourning can be even more difficult. To ignore painful or ambivalent memories is to prevent yourself from healing. You will need someone who can non-judgmentally explore any painful memories with you. If you repress or deny these memories, you risk carrying an underlying sadness or anger into your future.

In my experience, remembering the past makes hoping for the future possible. Your future will become open to new experiences only to the extent that you embrace the past.

A SURVIVOR SPEAKS:

"There were some great times and there were some really bad times. I found out I had to work with both the good memories and the bad. I also had to mourn for so much of what I wish could have been."

EXPRESS YOURSELF: Go to *The Understanding Your Suicide Grief Journal* on p. 96.

MOURNING NEED 4: DEVELOP A NEW SELF-IDENTITY

Your personal identity, or self-perception, is the result of the ongoing process of establishing a sense of who you are. Part of your self-identity comes from the relationships you have with other people. When someone with whom you have a relationship dies, your self-identity, or the way you see yourself, naturally changes.

You may have gone from being a "wife" or "husband" to a "widow" or "widower." You

Now I realize: I knew myself so little. This death has forced me to become reacquainted with myself. I must slow down and listen.

may have gone form being a "parent" to a "bereaved parent." The way you define yourself and the way society defines you is changed. As one woman said, "I used to have a husband and was part of a couple. Now I'm not only single, but a single parent and a widow… I hate that word. It makes me sound like a lonely spider."

A death often requires you to take on new roles that had been filled by the person who died. After all, someone still has to take out the garbage, buy the groceries, and balance the checkbook. You confront your changed identity every time you do something that used to be done by the person who died. This can be very hard work and, at times, can leave you feeling very drained of emotional, physical, and spiritual energy.

You may occasionally feel child-like as you struggle with your changing identity. You may feel a temporarily heightened dependence on others as well as feelings of helplessness, frustration, inadequacy, and fear. These feelings can be overwhelming and scary, but they are actually a natural response to this important need of mourning.

As you address this need, be certain to keep other major changes to a minimum if at all possible. Now is not the time for a major move or addition to the house. Your energy is already depleted. Don't deplete it even more by making significant changes and taking on too many tasks.

Remember—do what you need to do in order to survive, at least for now, as you try to re-anchor yourself. To be dependent on

When I have a commitment and longing to find my changed self, I have an alternative to the constant, blinding pain of the loss. Discovering my changed me clears a space to discover new life. I have something to turn toward instead of away from. I have something to cry out for that releases my inner tension. I have something that is authentic, real: It is the life that breaks through my loneliness, with a direction and power of its own. Welcome home.

others as you struggle with a changed identity does not make you weak, bad, or inferior. Your self-identity has been assaulted. Be compassionate with yourself. Accept the support of others.

Many people discover that as they work on this need, they ultimately discover some positive aspects of their changed self-identity. You may develop a renewed confidence in yourself. You may develop an assertive part of your identity that empowers you to go on living even though you continue to feel a sense of loss. (To learn more about the self-identity changes that come with grief, see Touchstone Ten.)

A SURVIVOR SPEAKS:

"It took me some time to figure out who I would be without her. I'd always been a husband, now I was a widower and a survivor of a suicide death. Wow—that was so much for me to take in. So I'm glad I had the support group friends who helped me with this."

EXPRESS YOURSELF: Go to *The Understanding Your Suicide Grief Journal* on p. 102.

MOURNING NEED 5: SEARCH FOR MEANING

When someone you love takes his or her own life, you naturally question the meaning and purpose of life. You probably will question your philosophy of life and explore religious and spiritual values as you work on this need. You may discover yourself searching for meaning in your continued living as you ask "how?" and "why?" questions. "How could God let this happen?" "Why did this happen now, in this way?" The death reminds you of your lack of control. It can leave you feeling powerless.

"Suicide is often judged to be an essentially selfish act. Perhaps it is. But the Bible warns us not to judge, if we ourselves hope to escape judgment. And I believe this is one area where that Biblical command especially should be heeded."

Norman Vincent Peale

As Edward K. Rynearson wisely noted following his wife Julie's death to suicide, "While religious or spiritual concepts might have prepared me for Julie's death, they could not prepare me for her violent dying. There is no spiritual belief or religion, despite any scripture or hymn or sermon, that finds order or meaning in a violent death." Yes, as he discovered, suicide can naturally complicate this search for meaning need. It can throw

I must encounter my questions, my doubts, my fears. There is richness in these domains. As I explore them, I don't reinforce my tensions but instead release them. In this way I transcend my grief and discover new life beyond anything my heart could ever have comprehended. Oh, the gentleness of new life.

your spiritual and/or religious life into disarray. It disrupts any kind of spiritual rhythm you may have been experiencing in your life. So, I plead with you: Be patient with yourself and repeat the mantra "No rewards for speed!"

After all, the person who died was a part of you. This death means you mourn a loss not only outside of yourself, but inside of yourself as well. At times, overwhelming sadness and loneliness may be your constant companions. You may feel that when this person died, part of you died with him or her. And now you are faced with finding some meaning in going on with your life even though you may often feel so empty.

This death calls for you to confront your own spirituality. You may doubt your faith and have spiritual conflicts and questions racing through your head and heart. This is normal and part of your journey toward renewed living.

I deserve to be proud of my search for meaning in life after the death of someone I love. Grief confronts me with the reality that life is now. Today. I can demonstrate the value of the lives of those who have died by living fully.

You might feel distant from your God or Higher Power, even questioning the very existence

149

of God. You may rage at your God. Such feelings of doubt are normal. Remember—mourners often find themselves questioning their faith for months before they rediscover meaning in life. But be assured: It can be done, even when you don't have all the answers.

Early in grief, allow yourself to openly mourn without pressuring yourself to have answers to profound meaning of life questions. Move at your own pace as you recognize that allowing yourself to hurt and find continued meaning to live are not mutually exclusive. More often, your need to mourn and your need to find meaning in your continued living will blend into each other, with the former very slowly giving way to the latter as healing occurs.

In my experience, the grief that comes with suicide demands that you dose the pain as you do this search for meaning work. In other words, befriending your pain is only a part of the healing. Without nourishing your need to search for meaning that invites you to go on living, the pain can eat away at you, leaving you feeling naked in the world. I have seen this happen when there is what I call a lack of nourishment surrounding the search for meaning. So, I say search away, and as you do, remember someone very wise once reminded me that "the heart of faith is believing one is never alone." Please don't allow yourself to feel alone in your search. Find compassionate companions who will accompany you on this wilderness journey.

A SURVIVOR SPEAKS:

"Faith has always been a big part of my life. This suicide death brought me some 'whys?' that left me having words with God. The good news is that I found out he could take my questions, and I was able to search. The search led me to find renewal, and while I'll always miss John, my best testimony is to live as well as I can from a place of purpose...and that is just what I have been able to do."

EXPRESS YOURSELF: Go to *The Understanding Your Suicide Grief Journal* on p. 104.

MOURNING NEED 6: LET OTHERS HELP YOU— NOW AND ALWAYS

The quality and quantity of understanding support you get during your work of mourning will have a major influence on your capacity to heal. You cannot—nor should you try to—do this alone. Drawing on the experiences and encouragement of friends, fellow mourners, or professional counselors is not a weakness but a healthy human need. And because mourning is a process that takes place over time, this support must be available months and even years after the suicide death of someone in your life.

> I heal, in part, by allowing others to express their love for me. By choosing to invite others into my journey, I move toward health and healing. If I hide from others, I hide from healing.

Unfortunately, because our society places so much value on the ability to "carry on," "keep your chin up," and "keep busy," many bereaved people are abandoned shortly after the event of the death. "It's best not to talk about death," "It's over and done with," and "It's time to get on with your life" are the types of messages directed at grieving people that sometimes still dominate, particularly when suicide is the cause of the death. Obviously, these messages encourage you to deny or repress your grief rather than express it.

If you know people who consider themselves supportive yet offer you these kinds of mourning-avoiding messages, you'll need to look to others for truly helpful support. People who see your mourning as something that should be overcome instead of experienced will not help you heal.

To be truly helpful, the people in your support system must appreciate the impact this death has had on you. They must understand that in order to heal, you must be allowed— even encouraged—to mourn long after the death. And they must encourage you to see mourning not as an enemy to be vanquished but as a necessity to be experienced as a result of having loved.

Healing in your grief journey will depend not only on your inner resources but also on your surrounding support system. Your sense of who you are and where you are with your healing process comes, in part, from the care and response of people close to you. One of the important sayings of The Compassionate Friends, an international organization of grieving parents, is "You need not walk alone." I might add, "You cannot walk alone." You will probably discover, if you haven't already, that you can benefit from a connectedness that comes from people who also have had a suicide death in their lives. Support groups, where people come together and share the common bond of experience, can be invaluable in helping you and your grief and supporting your need to mourn long after the event of the death.

I need not instinctively know what to do or how to be with my grief. I can reach out to others who have walked this path before. I must learn that to ultimately heal, I must touch and be touched by the experiences of those who have gone before me. These people can offer me hope, inner strength, and the gift of love.

You will learn more about support groups and how to create support systems for yourself later in this book. Right now, remind yourself that you deserve and need to have understanding people around you who allow you to feel your grief long after society deems appropriate.

A SURVIVOR SPEAKS:

"I cannot express how helpful it has been to make use of certain friends who have been understanding and supportive. My true friends and my support group have held my hand and walked with me from the start...and, to show their true wisdom, they realize there is no set finish line I am supposed to reach."

EXPRESS YOURSELF: Go to *The Understanding Your Suicide Grief Journal* on p. 107.

JOURNEYING WITH THE SIX NEEDS

I have been a grief companion to hundreds of survivors to suicide, and I've found that mourners are often helped by the concept of the six central needs of mourning. There is a lot of information in this book, but if you were to slowly commit to memory one small piece of information, I would recommend that it be the six needs of mourning. Simply, upholding and fulfilling these six needs will help you heal. I would also encourage you to revisit this chapter time and again in the future and review your progress in meeting these needs. Now, allow me to turn your attention toward the vital need to nurture yourself during this wilderness experience.

Touchstone Seven

NURTURE YOURSELF

*"Getting better means being patient with oneself
when progress is slow… It means finding safe,
supportive persons with whom to share the pain."*
Janice Harris Lord

As you have without a doubt discovered, when you experience
the death of someone from suicide, you have some very special
needs. Perhaps one of the most important special needs right
now is to be compassionate with yourself—to honor this season
of tenderness in your life. In fact, the word "compassion" means
"with passion." Caring for and about yourself with passion is
self-compassion.

This Touchstone is a gentle reminder to be kind to yourself as
you journey through the wilderness of your grief. Be gentle with
yourself. You are naturally fragile and vulnerable. You can give
attention to your wounds by making decisions that ultimately
contribute to your healing. Be assured that there will come a time
when your grief will not be overwhelming and when you really
do live once more. In the meantime, please allow me the honor
of trying to help you with your self-care needs.

If you were embarking on a hike of many days through the mountains of Colorado, would you dress scantily, carry little water, and push yourself until you dropped? Of course not. You would prepare carefully and proceed cautiously. You would take care of yourself because if you didn't, you could die. The consequence of not taking care of yourself as you grieve and mourn this death can be equally devastating.

Over many years of walking with hundreds of people in the wilderness of suicide grief, I have discovered that many of us are hard on ourselves during this time in our lives. Yet, good self-care is essential to your survival. Practicing good self-care doesn't mean you are feeling sorry for yourself, being selfish, or being self-indulgent; rather it means you are creating conditions that allow you to integrate the transformation that this suicide brings into your heart and soul.

As you well know by now, you are not the same person you were prior to this death entering into your life. If your experience is anything like mine, it is life-changing. You are not the same person you were when you entered the wilderness. You are *transformed*. As I will remind you again in Touchstone Ten, transformation literally means an entire change in form. While most of us would never seek out the kind of change we encounter, you will likely grow in your understanding, in your compassion, and in your love for your fellow human beings.

I truly believe that in nurturing yourself, in allowing yourself the time and loving attention you need to journey safely and deeply through the wilderness of suicide grief, you can and will find meaning in your continued living. I imagine you have heard the words, "Blessed are those who mourn, for they shall be comforted." I might add, "Blessed are those who learn self-compassion during times of profound grief, for they shall go on to discover continued meaning in life."

Remember that compassionate self-care fortifies you during your grief experience, an experience that leaves you profoundly affected and deeply changed. Above all, self-care is about self-acceptance. When you recognize that self-care begins with yourself, you no longer think of those around you as being totally responsible for your well-being.

The grief that comes with a suicide death invites you to embrace each precious moment of life, and to care deeply for your family and friends. Suicide grief invites you to find hidden treasures everywhere—a child's toothless smile, a beautiful sunrise, the smell of fresh flowers, a friend's gentle touch. In caring for yourself and tending to your special needs right this moment, you will go on to discover the capacity to live your life with purpose and meaning every moment of every day.

NURTURING YOURSELF IN FIVE IMPORTANT REALMS

When you have special needs, a helpful framework for nurturing yourself is the consideration of five important areas:

- Physical

- Emotional

- Cognitive

- Social

- Spiritual

What follows is an introduction to each of these areas. You will then be invited to go to your companion journal and express how you see yourself doing in each area. You will be able to affirm where you are doing excellent self-care and plan to make some changes in those areas you discover you may be lacking. I hope you will find this self-care framework helpful to you. Let's begin.

The Physical Realm

Your body may be letting you know it feels distressed. Actually, one literal definition of the word "grievous" is "causing physical suffering." You may be shocked by how much your body responds to the impact of your loss.

Among the most common physical responses to loss are troubles with sleeping and low energy. You may have difficulty getting to sleep. Perhaps even more commonly, you may wake up early in the morning and have trouble getting back to sleep. During your grief journey, your body needs more rest than usual. You may also find yourself getting tired more quickly, sometimes even at the start of the day.

Sleeping normally after a loss would be unusual. If you think about it, sleeping is the primary way in which we release control. When someone you love takes his or her own life, you feel a loss of control. You don't want to lose any more control by sleeping. The need to stay awake sometimes relates to the fear of additional losses; therefore, you may stay awake because you want to prevent more loss. Some grieving people have even taught me that they stay awake hoping not to miss the person who died in case he or she returns. If you have this experience, be assured you are not crazy. It is a normal part of searching and yearning for the person who died.

Muscle aches and pains, shortness of breath, feelings of emptiness in your stomach, tightness in your throat or chest, digestive problems, sensitivity to noise, heart palpitations, queasiness, nausea, headaches, increased allergic reactions, changes in appetite, weight loss or gain, agitation, and generalized tension—these are all ways your body may react to the death of someone loved.

If you have a chronic existing health problem, it may become worse. The stress of grief can suppress your immune system and make you more susceptible to physical problems.

Right now you may not feel in control of how your body is responding. Your body is communicating with you about the stress you are experiencing!

"And no one ever told me about the laziness of grief."
C.S. Lewis

Keep in mind, however, that in the majority of instances, the physical symptoms described above are normal and temporary.

Good self-care is important at this time. Your body is the house you live in. Just as your house requires care and maintenance to protect you from the outside elements, your body requires that you honor it and treat it with respect. The quality of your life ahead depends on how you take care of your body today. The lethargy of grief you are probably experiencing is a natural mechanism intended to slow you down and encourage you to care for your body.

And be certain to talk out your grief. Many grieving people have taught me that if they avoid or repress talking about the death, their bodies will begin to express their grief for them.

Caring For Your Physical Self

The following guidelines of good health are good counsel for anyone, but especially for those encountering the death of someone precious to suicide. While this is by no means an all-inclusive list, it should help you in your efforts to care for your physical self.

Stay Fluid

When you experience grief and loss, the mechanism in your body that lets you know when you are thirsty often shuts down. So, you will be well served to remind yourself to drink lots of water—at least six to eight glasses (10 to 12 ounces each) every day. Think of water as the oil that lubricates the body. Water (I often call it the very best fluid in the world) carries oxygen, nutrients, and hormones to your cells and eliminates waste products via the bloodstream and your lymphatic system. Remaining well hydrated also means having better digestion and less dry skin. Also, keep in mind that caffeinated and alcoholic drinks dehydrate you, so consider eliminating, or, at the very least, limiting, your intake.

Rest, Relax, and Renew

To experience grief invites you to suspend and slow down, not speed up and keep busy. So, right now you need to build in time each day to experience some rest, relaxation, and renewal. Some people might tell you to keep busy, but odds are your body will try to tell you to slow down. You might also think you don't have time to do this, but right now, with your very special needs, you need to make time! Rest helps your body survive right now and helps begin to restore your spirit. So, stop "doing" and simply "be" as much as you possibly can right now.

Try to Sleep as Well as Possible

No doubt your normal sleep-pattern is disturbed right now. You are probably falling asleep only when totally exhausted and then waking up throughout the night. This is much more common for survivors of suicide than sleeping normally. Your "sleep rhythm" is thrown off right now. As you mourn this will improve, but don't think there is something wrong with you because you are not sleeping as you normally have in the past. Sleep is restorative, and if anyone needs restoration right now it is you. So, try the best you can to get some sleep and use tools to assist you in the process. For example, try to get to bed at a similar time each night and get up at a similar time each morning. Limit your caffeine and alcohol intake. If you're getting very little sleep or none at all, see your family physician immediately. You need energy to do the work of mourning, and if you are not getting any sleep, you will be grieving but not mourning.

Have a Compassionate Physician as Part of Your Self-Care Plan

As noted, your body is very vulnerable right now. You will be wise to have a caring physician who can help you monitor your special physical needs. He or she can assist you in monitoring what your body is telling you about the demand it is experiencing. Be sure to tell your physician about the death; it is critical information if he or she is to be able to help you at this time. Think of your doctor as a kind of coach—a trained professional—who can help you care for your body that houses your spirit. He or she can also be an "encourager" during this difficult time in your life. Ask your doctor to help you remember to get some form of daily exercise that will help have a calming effect on your body, mind, and spirit. If you don't already have a trusted physician in your corner, get some help finding one right now and work to create a health-partnership.

Laugh When You Have an Opportunity

It turns out that humor is good medicine for your body, mind, and spirit. Research demonstrates that laughter stimulates chemicals in the brain that actually suppress stress-related hormones. Also, respiration and circulation are both enhanced through laughter.

In your grief, you may not feel like laughing very much right now. But as the journey progresses, find ways to build laughter into your life. You might go to a live comedy show, rent a movie that makes you laugh, or spend time with your funniest friend.

I hope the above guidelines related to physical self-care will help you take good care of your health. Knowing more about the needs of your body can help you design a program that best meets your unique needs. You will receive immediate results and create waves of positive energy. A personal commitment to your health paves the way for healthy self-care in the other four domains outlined below. Just as your life is being transformed right now, you can also transform your body and re-ignite your divine spark—that which gives your life meaning and purpose.

EXPRESS YOURSELF: Go to *The Understanding Your Suicide Grief Journal* on p. 112.

The Emotional Realm

We explored in Touchstone Four a multitude of emotions that are often part of grief and mourning. These emotions reflect that you have special needs that require support from both outside yourself and inside yourself. Becoming familiar with the terrain of these emotions

"The emotions may be endless. The more we express them, the more we may have to express."
E.M. Forster

and practicing the self-care guidelines noted can and will help you authentically mourn and heal in small doses over time. The important thing to remember is that we honor our emotions when we give attention to them.

Acknowledge and Express

As your experience has probably taught you, there are many feelings to be felt and expressed during this very difficult time. Feelings that go unexpressed often become painful attitudes that are self-defeating. For example, fears not expressed often become avoidance; hurt not expressed often becomes permanent sadness; anger not expressed often becomes depression.

All feelings have some purpose. They are your teachers. So, you must find a safe place and people with whom to express them. While you have to be selective about who you express your feelings to (even some close friends will not want to experience the depth of your feelings), they do need to be converted from grief (internal) to mourning (external). Odds are this is going to be done with a counselor, a support group, select friends, or a combination of them. This is simply a gentle reminder to be sure you honor the emotions that are part of your journey.

Keep a Journal

If this is an avenue that fits, keeping a journal can be a gentle, self-compassionate way to nurture your emotions of grief and loss. The process of writing down what you are experiencing invites you to pause and be conscious of what you are feeling and thinking. Journaling gives you that time and honors the need for you to take your inner thoughts and feelings of grief (your internal response to loss) and convert them to mourning (the shared social response to loss). Journaling, while private and independent, still allows and encourages you to express your grief outside of yourself. Obviously, if you are using the companion journal to this text, you are making use of the tool related to your emotional realm.

Allow Yourself to Cry

As you learned under misconceptions about grief (see p. 45), tears are a natural cleansing and healing mechanism. They rid your body of stress chemicals. What's more, tears are a form of mourning, and they are sacred! You may find yourself crying at unexpected times or places. If you need to, excuse yourself or retreat somewhere private. Or better yet, go ahead and cry openly and honestly, unashamed of your tears of overwhelming grief. Do keep in mind that not everyone is a crier, but if you are, crying can be a great avenue to nurture your emotional self.

Listen to Meaningful Music

Music, perhaps more than any other external experience, has the capacity to bring you home to yourself and to restore your broken heart. Beautiful music can communicate to you on many different levels. Music can take you to your favorite place or to another world.

Music transforms you, taking you to a safe place in your soul, helping you feel that you and the world around you are filled with grace and peace. Music can uplift your mood, soothe you when you are agitated, and open you to harmony, beauty, love, and generosity.

Beautiful music that nurtures your being is by its very nature healing. It restores and relaxes you in ways beyond words. Music allows you to access spirit through sound. Music can infuse your body, mind, and spirit, and bring an inner calmness that comforts your grief-filled nerves. Music encourages you to express your grief from the inside to mourning on the outside. Music is an invitation to feel whatever you feel—sometimes even paradoxical emotions, such as happiness and sadness at once.

Sit in Silence and Solitude

The mystery of grief invites you to honor the need for periods of silence and solitude. As you quiet yourself, you sustain an open heart and a gentle spirit. Mother Teresa often said, "The beginning of prayer is silence." You may not have access to a cloistered monastery, a walk in the woods, or a stroll on the beach, but you do have the capacity to quiet yourself. Consciously hush yourself and place trust in the peace you help initiate. As you sit with silence, you acknowledge that you value the need to suspend, slow down, and turn inward as part of the grief journey. Giving attention to the instinct to mourn from the inside out requires that you befriend silence and respect how vital it is to your healing journey.

Many of the symptoms of grief are invitations to the need for silence and solitude. Disorganization, confusion, searching and yearning, and the lethargy of grief try to slow you down and invite a need for you to savor silence. Yes, astutely observed, "For many afflictions, silence is the best remedy." Silence contains the ingredients that can bring some peace in the midst of the wilderness. The forces of grief weigh heavy on your heart. Silence serves to lift up your heart and create much-needed space to give attention to your grief.

EXPRESS YOURSELF: Go to *The Understanding Your Suicide Grief Journal* on p. 113.

The Cognitive Realm

Your mind is the intellectual ability to think, absorb information, make decisions, and reason logically. Without doubt, you have special needs in the cognitive realm of your grief experience. Just as your body and emotions let you know you have experienced being torn apart, your mind has also, in effect, been torn apart.

Thinking normally after the suicide death of someone precious to you would be very unlikely. Don't be surprised if

"Thinking is the talking of the soul with itself."
Plato

you struggle with short-term memory problems, have trouble making even simple decisions, and think you may be going crazy. Essentially, your mind is in a state of disorientation and confusion.

When Possible, Do Not Make Impulsive Major Decisions During This Time

While it can be helpful to have goals to help you look to a brighter future, it can be a mistake to make too many changes too quickly. The grief following a suicide death often sets off "fight or flight" responses. Sometimes, in an effort to get away from pain, you can be tempted to make rash decisions. Some people move to a new city or quit their jobs. Some people jump into new relationships too quickly.

Typically these changes are soon regretted. They often end up compounding feelings of loss and complicating healing as well as creating staggering new headaches.

If at all possible (and I realize it isn't always possible), avoid making additional major changes for a while. After all, you are already experiencing overwhelming grief with additional layers of change and loss. You cannot run away from the pain, so don't make it worse by trying to.

Of course, sometimes you may be forced to make a significant change in your life after a death. Financial realities may force you to sell your home, for example. In these cases, know that you are doing what you must and try to trust as best you can that everything will work out.

Simplify Your Life

During the cognitive confusion of grief, it is easy to get overwhelmed by the daily tasks and commitments you have. Profound loss can really make you take stock of what is important in your life. If you can rid yourself of some of these extraneous burdens, you'll have more time for healing.

What are some things that might be overburdening you right now? For example, have your name taken off junk mailing lists, don't make yourself stressed out because your house isn't always sparkling clean and neat, and stop attending optional meetings you don't look forward to.

Write Things Down

Your short-term memory is impaired right now. So, help yourself out and write things down. A brief daily to-do list can help you focus during this difficult time. (Oh, and then make a list of where you put your list because you will probably forget where you put it. I hope that brought a little laugh to you! A little laughter is good for your soul right now.)

Say No and Set Limits

When your cognitive capacity and physical energy are compromised, you may lack the psychic energy to participate in activities you used to find pleasurable. It's okay to say no when you're asked to help with a project or attend a party.

Give a brief phone call to people who have invited you and simply thank them for the invite but say no. You don't need to feel obligated to go on and on and explain why. You have the right to say no. But be sure to also ask to be invited next time. Your rebuffs may be taken as permanent nos if you don't help others understand that your needs and boundaries will likely change over time.

Do recognize that you will not be able to keep saying no forever, though. There will be some events you won't want to miss. Don't miss out on life's most joyful celebrations. However, trust your sense of when the time is right for you to rejoin in the occasions.

Practice Patience

Your normal cognitive abilities take longer to return after a death than most people are aware. So, you need to be patient and gentle with yourself. Our society, which promotes hyper-living, is constantly trying to speed things up. However, your confused, slow-thinking mind has wisdom and is trying to slow you down because this is what you need right now. Patience is the ability to endure or to persevere with a calm heart during difficult moments. So, take each and every opportunity you have right now to practice being patient with yourself and your grief journey. Keep repeating the mantra, "No rewards for speed."

Practicing patience opens your mind and heart to the present moment and allows healing and joy into your life.

Take Some Time Off Work

If at all possible (and I realize it isn't always, especially in times of economic hardship), there is no time like now for you to take some extended time away from the demands of your work life. Talk to your employer about taking off some additional time or using some vacation time. Some companies will grant extended leaves of absence or sabbaticals in some situations.

If you simply cannot take off additional time, try not to take on new challenges that will further task your concentration and memory right now. Instead of taking on more, just try to survive in your workplace for a while. Over time, your focus will return, and you will be able to once again perform well in your job.

EXPRESS YOURSELF: Go to *The Understanding Your Suicide Grief Journal* on p. 115.

The Social Realm

The suicide death of someone you love has resulted in a very real disconnection from the world around you. When you reach out and connect with your family and friends, you are beginning to reconnect. By being aware of the larger picture, one that includes all the people in your life, you gain some perspective. You recognize you are part of a greater whole, and that recognition can empower you. You open up your heart to love again when you reach out to others. Your link to family, friends, and community is vital for your sense of well-being and belonging.

"Friendship doubles our joy and divides our grief."
Swedish Proverb

If you don't nurture the warm, loving relationships that still exist in your life, you will probably continue to feel disconnected and isolated. You may even withdraw into your own small world and grieve but not mourn. Isolation can then become the barrier that keeps your grief from softening over time. You will begin to die while you are still alive. Allow your friends and family to nurture you. Let them in and rejoice in the connection.

Caring for Your Social Self

The following are some practical ideas to help you care for your social self during your grief journey.

Recognize That Your Friendships Will Probably Change

You may well find that some friends seem to go away during this time in your life. Know that just like you, your friends are doing the best they can. Don't be surprised if some of your friends cannot even talk with you about the death. For some, your reality is a threat to their potential reality. Instead of acknowledging their own fears, they feel a need to go away and not talk to you. Yes, this is sad, but often true.

Some people, including members of your family and friendship system, may not be able to be present to you in the wilderness of your grief. Suicide makes some people feel very awkward and uncomfortable. They may not even be conscious of this reaction, but nonetheless, it affects their ability to support you. Limit your time around family and friends who cannot be supportive to you.

The best way for you to respond in the face of strained relationships is to be proactive and honest. Even though you are the one who is in the wilderness, you may need to be the one to phone your family and friends to keep in touch. When you talk to them, be honest. Tell them how you're really feeling and that you appreciate any support they can provide you. If you find that certain people can't support you right now, stick to lighter topics with them and look for support from people whom you learn are capable of giving it. Put yourself in the company of warm-hearted, non-judgmental people who help you feel accepted and cared for.

Turn To Select Family Members

If you ever needed to embrace the gift of having some loving, caring family members, it is right now. Your friends may come and go, but family, as they say, is forever. If you're emotionally close to members of your family, you're probably already reaching out to them for support. Allow them to be there for you. Let them in.

If you're not emotionally close to your family, perhaps now is the time to open closed doors. You may be surprised what happens when you call a family member you haven't spoken to for a while. If possible, get in the car or on a plane and make a long-overdue visit. Don't feel bad if you have to be the initiator; instead expend your energy by writing that first letter or making that first phone call.

I would gently help you understand that if the person who has taken his or her own life was within your family, your family becomes a "pressure cooker," meaning that you all have a high need to feel understood and little capacity to be understanding of each other right now. Because of this natural dynamic after a suicide death within your family, you will probably be well served to seek some support outside of your family members. It doesn't mean they don't care about you; it is just that everyone is running on empty right now. In other words, adjust any expectations you might have that your family is closer right now and allow yourself some outside support. Of course, if your family is closer right now, celebrate that you may be the exception to the rule.

Identify Two People You Can Turn To Anytime
You Need A Friend

You may have many people who care about you but few people who can truly be present to you at this time in your life. Identify and stay conscious of two people whom you believe can and will be there for you in the coming weeks and months. Have gratitude for their support and let them know how much it means to you.

Reach Out To Counselors, Support Groups, And Additional Resources

Sometimes you need more structured support than your friends and family can provide. To seek social support from these domains is the very heart of Touchstone Eight, "Reach Out for Help." Please see this information on p. 182.

Find A Way To Connect To Others Or To Nature Each And Every Day

When you are in the wilderness of grief and impacted in this social area of your life, it may be difficult to look forward to each day when you are experiencing pain and sadness. So, to counterbalance your normal and necessary mourning, plan something you enjoy doing and that will help you to connect to others every day.

You might also find it is restorative to spend some time out in nature. The sound of a bird singing or the awesome presence of an old tree can help put things in perspective.

Some people (I know I do) find that being near water has a natural healing quality during times of overwhelming grief and loss. The gentle feeling of ocean waves washing up on the shoreline, the trickling of a mountain stream, the serenity of a quiet pond—all these aquatic sensations can offer comfort. Water can soothe the body and the soul.

If water doesn't work for you, try a mountain. Hiking on a mountain pass can be an invigorating, soul-searching experience. There is something about mountains that invites you to discover the essentials within your spirit and the spirit of the world around you. Those of you who don't live near mountains will also find solace in a park, a forest, a wetland, or any other natural setting.

EXPRESS YOURSELF: Go to *The Understanding Your Suicide Grief Journal* on p. 118.

The Spiritual Realm

Let me assure you that I realize the word spiritual has many different meanings to different people. The survivors of suicide I have companioned have taught me that each person's spiritual journey is unique and sustained by his or her individual beliefs and values. The suicide death of someone precious to you becomes part of the *mystery* and is not something you can quickly and easily understand. You might find it helpful to remember that *mystery* was the ancient name for God.

For our purpose here, I think of spirituality as the collection of beliefs about our existence. Obviously, when someone takes his or her own life, you are invited into some spiritual questions for which there are no easy answers: "Why did this happen?" "Will my life be worth living again?" You may feel a loss of faith or doubt or feel distant from any sense of spirituality. Yes, sometimes the irony of believing involves doubting, and suicide can naturally engage you in doubting. That is why, if I could, I would encourage all of us when we are in the midst of the grief that accompanies suicide to put down "Nurture my spirit" first on our daily to-do lists.

> *"When we lose God, we do not lose the yearning for God... Loss is the platform on which we build a deeper, sturdier faith."*
> David Wolpe

My own personal sense of spirituality anchors me, allowing me to put life into perspective. For me, spirituality involves a sense of connection to all things in nature, God, and the world at large. I recognize that, for some, contemplating a spiritual life in the midst of the many faces of suicide grief can be difficult and, at times, perhaps even feeling impossible. Yet, in my experience, once you have discovered your spiritual core, you will have an undergirding strength that will support you in your wilderness experience.

Like myself, you probably recognize that spirituality and religiosity are not synonymous. In some people's lives they overlap completely; their religious lives are their spiritual lives. Other people have a rich spiritual life with few or no ties to organized religion. Obviously, each of us defines our own spirituality in the depths of our own hearts and minds. The paths we choose will be our own, discovered through self-examination, reflection, and spiritual transformation.

I do personally believe that even in your grief, you can still befriend *hope* (if I didn't believe this I could not function in my helping role at my Center for Loss or support survivors of suicide deaths), and that even the most ordinary moment can feed your soul. In some ways, spirituality is anchored in faith, which is expecting some goodness even in the worst of times. It is not about fear, which is expecting the worst even in the best of times. Spirituality reminds you that you can and will integrate losses into your life, that there is goodness in others, and that there are many pathways to Heaven.

If you have doubts about your capacity to connect with your spirituality, your religion, or your God right now, try to approach the world with the openness of a child. Embrace the support you can experience

"To understand the restoration of the soul means we have to make spirituality a more serious part of everyday life."
Thomas Moore

from the simple things in life: the unexpected kindness of a stranger; a sunrise or sunset; the rustle of the wind in the trees. Even in the face of your devastating loss, you can and will find yourself discovering the essentials within your soul and spirit of the world around you.

Caring For Your Spiritual Self

The following are some practical ideas to help you care for your spiritual self during this time of your life.

Nurture Your Spirit

Your spirit has been deeply injured by the death of someone in your life to suicide. Nurturing your spirit relates to caring for that part of yourself that is transcendent. You spirit speaks to you

with inner messages and invites you to surround yourself with
positive regard. Nurturing your spirit means giving attention to
your underlying beliefs and values.

You can care for your spirit in ways ranging from inspirational
reading to listening to or playing music, being with those you
feel support from, walking in the woods, strolling on the beach,
climbing a mountain, or spending time in the company of wise,
compassionate people of any spiritual path.

Without doubt, mourning a death to suicide is a spiritual journey
of the heart and soul. Traumatic grief invites you to consider why
people live, why people die, and what gives life meaning and
purpose. These are the most spiritual questions we have language
to form. No one can "give" you spirituality from the outside in;
you have to "give" it to yourself from the inside out. Nurturing
your spirit is one way to do just that.

Sit in the Sanctuary of Stillness

Sitting in stillness with your grief will help you honor the deeper
voices of quiet wisdom that come forth from within you. As
Rainer Maria Rilke observed, "Everything is gestation and then
bringing forth." In honoring your need to be still, you rest for the
journey.

Personal times of stillness are a spiritual necessity. A lack of
stillness hastens confusion and disorientation and results in a
waning of your spirit. Stillness restores your life force. Grief is
only transformed when you honor the quiet forces of stillness.

Yes, integration of grief is borne out of stillness, not frantic
movement forward. When you halt any instinct to attempt to
"manage" your grief, other impulses such as grace, wisdom,
love, and truth come forth. Any frantic attempts to quickly
"move forward" or "let go" become counterproductive and
deplete an already-malnourished soul. It is through sitting with
your stillness that your soul is ever so slowly restored.

Go to Exile

Choosing to spend time alone is an essential self-nurturing spiritual practice. If affords you the opportunity to be unaffected by others' wants and needs. It is impossible to really know yourself if you never take time to withdraw from the demands of daily living. Alone time does not mean you are being selfish. Instead, you will experience rest and renewal in ways you otherwise would not. A lack of alone time produces heightened confusion and a muting of your life force. Your human spirit is naturally compassionate, and once you feel restored, your instinct to be kind and generous to those around you will be revitalized.

Even Jesus went to exile. He modeled the simple spiritual practice of rest and alone time as a natural, nourishing, and valuable companion to times of busyness. Jesus would sometimes send people away, disappear without warning or explanation, and retreat to a place of rest. If Jesus went to exile, so can you!

Within your exiled time and space will evolve the insights and blessings that come to the surface only in stillness and with time. Schedule alone time on a regular basis. Don't shut out your family and friends altogether, but do answer the call for contemplative solitude.

Start Each Day With A Prayer Or Meditation

For many people in the wilderness of grief, waking up in the morning can be a difficult part of the day. It's as if each time you awaken, you confront the realization of the loss of your relationship.

You may find that you can help set the tone for your day by praying or meditating. Prayer and meditation are some of the easiest spiritual practices you can do any time, any place, any way. You might not only experience some wisdom that comes from these practices, but also experience the peace that comes from spending quiet, reflective time with God. Of course, if you are mad at God you can use some of this time to openly express what you think and feel. The good news is that God can receive any anger you might have. And, keep in mind, having anger at God speaks of having a relationship with God.

Prayer can be a natural avenue for mourning in that it involves talking your thoughts and feelings through and expressing them outside of yourself. Even when you pray silently, you're forming words for your thoughts and feelings and you're offering up those words to a presence outside of yourself. If you are so inclined, do keep in mind that many places of worship have prayer lists that you can be put on. Call yours and ask that your name be added to the prayer list. On worship days, the whole congregation will pray for you.

Some people think of prayer as a practice directed at petitioning God for what they want. Try viewing prayer differently: See it as a practice that aims to change your life not by divine intervention, but by creating a more humble spirit in you. The purpose of prayer is to change you, not the circumstances surrounding your grief experience.

Create A Sacred Space of Sanctuary

Creating a sacred, safe place—a sanctuary—just for you may be one of the most loving ways you can help yourself at this time. Yes, you need the loving support of friends, family and community, but nurturing yourself during difficult times can also involve going to exile.

Whether it is indoors or out, give yourself a place for spiritual contemplation. The word *contemplate* means "to make space for the divine to enter." Think of your space, if only a simple room, as a place dedicated exclusively to the needs of the soul. Retreat to your space seven times a week and honor your journey through the wilderness of grief.

Celebrate A Sunrise

The sun is a powerful symbol of life and renewal. When was the last time you watched the sun rise? Do you remember being touched by its beauty and power? Plan an early morning experience where you can see the sun rise. Find a place that offers you a great view. You may need to go alone, or invite a supportive friend to share the dawn with you. Embrace your personal transformation and feel blessed by the dawning of a new day, a new life!

Know That You Are Loved

Love gives our lives meaning. Look around you for expressions of care and concern. There are people who love you and who want to be an important part of your support system.

Yes, some of those who love you may not know how to reach out to you, but they still love you. Reflect on the people who care about you and the ways in which your life matters. Open your heart and have gratitude for those who love you.

Find a Spiritual Director

A spiritual director or spiritual companion is someone who is trained in compassionate listening who will support you in your journey. You can find sources near you by going to www.sdiworld.org (Spiritual Directors International). Don't be afraid to try several directors until you find the person who connects with you.

Sigh

In Romans 8, it says that when there are not words for our prayer, the Spirits intervene and pray for us in sighs deeper than anything that can be expressed in words. Sigh deeply. Sigh whenever you feel like it. Each sigh is your prayer.

Spend Time in "Thin Places"

In the Celtic tradition, "thin places" are spots where the separation between the physical world and the spiritual world seem tenuous. They are places where the veil between Heaven and earth, between the holy and the everyday, are so thin that when we are near them, we intuitively sense the timeless, boundless spiritual world. There is a Celtic saying that Heaven and earth are only three feet apart, but in the thin places that distance is even smaller.

Thin places are usually outdoors, often where water and land meet or land and sky come together. You might find thin places on a riverbank, a beach, or a mountaintop. Go to a thin place to pray, to walk, or to simply sit in the presence of the holy.

If you find these spiritual practice suggestions helpful, you might also find my book *Healing Your Grieving Soul: 100 Spiritual Practices for Mourners* a useful resource.

EXPRESS YOURSELF: Go to *The Understanding Your Suicide Grief Journal* on p. 121.

Practicing Self-Compassion

We've discussed the five realms of self-care in grief: physical, emotional, cognitive, social, and spiritual. If you care for yourself "with passion" in all five realms, you will find your journey through the wilderness much more tolerable. So be good to yourself.

Finding others who will be good to you on your journey is also critically important. You can't walk this path alone. In the next chapter my hope is to help you construct a plan to reach out to others for help.

Touchstone Eight

REACH OUT FOR HELP

*"At times our light goes out and is rekindled
by a spark from another person."*
Albert Schweitzer

Surviving the death of someone precious in your life catapults
you into a wilderness experience filled with shock, disorientation
and confusion, and chaos. I recognize that reaching out for help
is more challenging than many people think. Early on in your
journey, you may be doing well to just breathe in and breathe
out, let alone make a thoughtful decision to get help from
friends, family, support groups, or professional caregivers.

I also recognize that I emphasized throughout this book that the
wilderness of your grief is *your* wilderness, and that in some
ways you have to find your own unique way through. But,
paradoxically, you also need companionship from time to time as
you journey. I believe that each and every one of us (obviously,
that includes *you*) who has experienced the death of someone to
suicide both needs and deserves the support, compassion, and
understanding of our fellow human beings. No, you need not,
and really cannot, walk alone in this wilderness!

Too often, integrating traumatic death into your life is delayed if you try to mend yourself before, and not after, seeking help from friends, family, caregivers, and I would also add God or your Higher Power. In large part, you invite your eventual healing by being willing to ask for help and being willing to receive help. For, in truth, you cannot heal alone and in isolation. Some survivors I have companioned have feared asking for help because they were too embarrassed, or too proud, or too angry to ask for help. Please don't allow this to happen to you.

You deserve a caring community of supportive people to wrap you in the cradle of unconditional love and support. You deserve companions who will walk beside you and provide you with divine momentum—affirmations that what you are doing is right and necessary for you and will lead to your eventual healing. Healing, in part, asks nothing of you other than your willingness to accept healing. Yet, again, allow me to gently remind you, *you cannot be healed alone and in isolation*!

Perhaps the most compassionate thing you can do for yourself at this vulnerable, overwhelming time is to reach out to others for help. Think of it this way: Grieving and mourning the death of someone precious to suicide is probably the hardest work you have ever done. And hard work is less burdensome when others lend a hand. You do *not* need people who want to walk in front of you and lead you down the path they think is right, nor do you need people who want to walk behind you and not be present to your pain. Instead, you do need people who are willing to learn from you and enter into your pain without a felt need to take it away.

You've heard me urge you over and over again in this book to seek out the support of the people in your life who are naturally good helpers. A few shoulders to cry on and some listening ears can make all the difference in the world. No, sharing your pain and loss with others won't make it disappear, but it will, over time, make it more bearable. Reaching out for help also connects you to other people and strengthens the bonds of love that make life worth living again.

Also, when you do ask for help, you have to open your heart and soul to be available to receive the help. I like to say the following to those I am honored to support in this journey: You have to *ask* for the help, *believe* you are deserving of the help, and then *receive* the help. So, I invite you to create a mantra: Ask – Believe – Receive! Oh, and when you do ask, you may want to release any tendency to try to control what you think your healing "ought," "should," or "must" look like. I have discovered a simple truth… you cannot always control your own healing. You might discover it from the most unexpected of persons, places, or experiences. So, I ask you to open to the miracle of healing your broken heart and wounded spirit!

WHERE TO TURN FOR HELP

While there is no one best place to turn for support, allow me to explore some of your options with you. Perhaps you can then be open to trying some of these out and see what the most comfortable options, or combinations of options, are for you.

Fellow Survivors

Perhaps, you have heard the saying, "United we stand, divided we fall." You may well find some of your most compassionate support from other suicide survivors. In their company, you can express your grief openly without fear of judgment. You will often discover you speak the same language and can instinctively retell your story as much as you need to. Instead of feeling any sense of being "shut down," you will be invited to "open up." And, as you open up, you will experience a genuine and authentic empathy that will inspire your awareness of the need to express your vulnerability without a filter.

"When we admit our vulnerability, we include others. If we deny it, we shut them out."

Mary Sarton

Selected Friends and Family

Keeping in mind the dynamics of the pressure-cooker phenomenon I described on p. 62, do realize that select friends and family members can often provide some of the support you need. The caring, warmth, and support of the "right" friends and family can go a long way in helping you. Sometimes, even a few compassionate friends and family who are gifted with effective listening ears can make all the difference in the world. Who can you discern has this capacity among your friends and family? Oh, and don't assume that everyone in your family and friendship system will be capable of loving and supporting you through this experience. Expand your network beyond these people to other sources of support.

Unfortunately, a suicide death lets you find out very quickly whom you can count on among your family and friends. Some *"A friend is one who walks in when others walk out."* Walter Winchell will simply not have any idea of what to say or do to support you. Some will disappear and you may not hear from them for a long time, if ever. Some will make awkward attempts to comfort you but will actually make things worse (see Dr. Wolfelt's rule of thirds, p. 185).

Fortunately, others will be there when you need them and create a safe place for you to express whatever you need to without any need to interpret or judge you in any way. When you do find these people among your friends and family, it becomes easier to ask for what you need from them. If you need to talk, call one of the people who will listen without telling you what you should think or feel. If you need something done, like cleaning your house, but don't have the energy to do it, call one of these people who will be more than willing to spend time helping you. Actually, you often do them a favor when you can tell them concrete things they can do to help you. Of course, let them know how much you appreciate their love and support. Remember—you are loved!

EXPRESS YOURSELF: Go to *The Understanding Your Suicide Grief Journal* on p. 126.

Support Groups

"Survivors share a special bond that is based on trust, not secrecy or shame."

Carla Fine

Another source you might consider is a support group of fellow travelers on this journey. Perhaps you have and are using this book as a resource for your support group framework. If so, I say thank you and bravo!

Support groups, where you come together and share the common bond of experience, can connect you to other people in deep and intimate ways. In these groups, each person shares his or her unique grief journey in a non-threatening, safe atmosphere. Over time, many participants report feeling like "family." Group members are usually very patient with you and your grief and encourage the sacred retelling of your story.

To find a suicide support group in your area, contact the American Association of Suicidology at 1-202-237-2280 or go to their website at www.suicidology.org. Another contact option is the American Foundation for Suicide Prevention at 1-888-333-2377 or go to their website at www.afsp.org. My Center for Loss will also be posting suicide support groups that evolve around this book at www.centerforloss.com. Or, you can give us a call at 970-226-6050 and we will try our best to help you locate a support group to companion you on your journey.

EXPRESS YOURSELF: Go to *The Understanding Your Suicide Grief Journal* on p. 126.

How to Know if You've Found a "Healthy" Support Group

Not all support groups will be helpful to you. Sometimes the group dynamic becomes unhealthy for one reason or another. Look for the following signs of a healthy support group.

1. Group members acknowledge that each person's grief is unique. They respect and accept both what members have in common and what is unique to each member.

2. Group members understand that grief is not a disease but rather a normal process without a specific timetable.

3. All group members are made to feel free to talk about their grief. However, if some decide to listen without sharing, their preference is respected.

4. Group members understand the difference between actively listening to what another person is saying and expressing their own grief. They make every effort not to interrupt when someone else is speaking.

5. Group members respect others' right to confidentiality. Thoughts, feelings, and experiences shared in the group are not made public.

6. Each group member is allowed equal time to speak; one or two people do not monopolize the group's time.

7. Group members don't give advice to each other unless it is asked for.

8. Group members recognize that thoughts and feelings are neither right, nor wrong. They listen with empathy to the thoughts and feelings of others without trying to change them.

EXPRESS YOURSELF: Go to *The Understanding Your Suicide Grief Journal* on p. 127.

Your Religious or Spiritual Community

Some survivors find loving support from their religious or spiritual community. The grief from suicide can potentially set you off on a spiritual pilgrimage. Search out and locate compassionate sources of support and understanding. Avoid any persons of faith who purport that those who complete suicide go to hell. Unfortunately, there are still a few of those people out there. I believe that a person's last act, suicide, no more defines his or her life than other acts throughout his or her lifetime. This last act is traumatic for you as a survivor, but I hope you agree with me that it doesn't negate the importance of other acts. We as humans are too complex to simplify into a single act. So, if you

Dr. Wolfelt's "Rule of Thirds"

In my own grief experiences and in the lives of people I have been privileged to counsel, I have discovered that in general, you can take all the people in your life and divide them into thirds when it comes to grief support.

One third of the people in your life will turn out to be neutral in response to your grief experience. They will neither help nor hinder you in your journey.

Another third of the people in your life will turn out to be harmful to you in your efforts to integrate the grief and loss into your life. While they are usually not setting out to intentionally harm you, they will judge you, give you unsolicited advice about what you should do, minimize your experience, "buck you up," or in general just try to pull you off your path to eventual healing and transcendence.

And the final third of people in your life will turn out to be truly supportive helpers. They will demonstrate a desire to understand you and the experience you are going through. They will demonstrate a willingness to be taught by you and recognize that you are the expert of your experience, not them. They will be willing to be involved in your pain and suffering without feeling the need to take it away from you. They will believe in your capacity to integrate this grief into your life and eventually go on to live a life of meaning and purpose.

Obviously, you want to seek out your friends, family, and caregivers who fall into the last third. They will be your confidants and momentum-givers on your journey. When you are in the wilderness of suicide grief, try to avoid that second third, for they will trip you up and cause you to fall. They may even light up a wildfire right there in the midst of your wilderness!

EXPRESS YOURSELF: Go to *The Understanding Your Suicide Grief Journal* on p. 128.

find someone of "faith" who does just that, look elsewhere for your spiritual support.

Fortunately, there are some excellent spiritual places and people who can and will help you get the support you deserve. Also, allow me to gently remind you that mourning openly and deeply is no more an indication of "weak" faith than of "strong" faith. Yes, as I like to say, "Blessed are those who mourn openly and honestly, for hopefully they will find support and compassion."

Churches, synagogues, and other spiritual groups offer a variety of resources that may be of help to you, ranging from individual counseling to classes, workshops, and support groups. While some of these programs are anchored in a specific religious tradition, many are open to people of any faith, not just members of the host organization.

Also, it is important to realize that not all of the suicide services offered by faith communities are spiritually based or faith-based; some are completely secular, the only connection being the physical space where meetings take place. Many of these programs are non-denominational and reach out in a way that honors diversity. Also, many of these programs are available for free or at a very low cost, accepting donations or waiving costs altogether if you cannot afford to pay.

If your religious faith or spirituality is a vital source of comfort to you, you may be well served to seek out sources of support in these kinds of settings. Again, just be a wise and discerning shopper. Find a place you feel at home, understood, and unjudged. Spiritual support may be just what you need to put things in perspective, get practical assistance, and restore your faith in a future filled with gratitude and hope.

EXPRESS YOURSELF: Go to *The Understanding Your Suicide Grief Journal* on p. 127.

Safe People: Three Fundamental Helping Roles

"I get by with a little help from my friends."
John Lennon

While there are a multitude of ways that people who care about you might reach out to help you, here are three important and fundamental helping roles. Effective helpers will help you:

Feel companioned during your journey. Those who companion you are willing and able to affirm your pain and suffering. They are able to sit with you and the feelings that surface as you walk through the wilderness. They are able to break through their separation from you and truly companion you where you are at this moment in time. They know that real compassion comes out of "walking with you," not ahead of you or behind you.

Encounter your feelings related to the suicide death. These are people who understand the need for you to tell your account of your grief experience. They gently invite you to tell your story and provide a safe place for you to openly express your many thoughts and feelings. Essentially, they give you an invitation to take any grief that is inside you and share it outside yourself.

Embrace hope. These are people around you who help you sustain the presence of hope—an expectation of good that is yet to be—given where you are in the middle of the wilderness of your grief. They do not force the concept of hope upon you but rather gently embody joy and hopefulness. They can be present to you and affirm your goodness, while all the time helping you trust in yourself that you can and will heal.

EXPRESS YOURSELF: Go to *The Understanding Your Suicide Grief Journal* on p. 128.

A Professional Counselor or Caregiver

A professional counselor may be a very helpful addition to your support system. There is no shame or weakness in seeing a counselor. On the contrary, it takes wisdom to realize you would benefit from this kind of help.

Since this is a naturally vulnerable time for you, however, you do need to use your discernment skills to find the right counselor for you. Try to find someone whom you connect and resonate with. You will know you may have found the right counselor when you feel safe, can be open and honest, and your spirit feels "at home."

In selecting a counselor (keep in mind they might have different job titles, ranging from psychologist to psychiatrist, social worker, family therapist or counselor), you have the right to ask questions. After all, you deserve someone who is best matched to your needs.

Training, Philosophy, Experience

As you explore your options, feel free to ask about the counselor's education and training. What degrees has she earned? What certificates or licenses does he hold? Is she certified in grief counseling? Reputable professionals will feel comfortable answering questions about their training, philosophy, and experience. Be certain the person you are seeing specializes in suicide-related issues. Even highly qualified professionals may not have experience working with suicide grief. If he or she hasn't worked in this area, keep looking. Of course, if you sense an uneasiness with exploring suicide grief, find someone else.

Relationship

While this is a very subjective area, the question is: Does the person seem like someone you would be able to work with effectively? Does her personality, answers to your questions and concerns, and office environment make you feel safe and respected? Do you sense that he genuinely cares about you as a human being and about the work you are going to be doing together? Essentially, do you feel comfortable with this person and sense that she can help you? If it does not feel right, then it is probably not right for you.

Some excellent counseling with the right person can give you insights and tools that will be invaluable to you during this difficult time in your life. A gentle course of counseling, with the right match for you, can be a life-changing experience and a vital step on your healing path.

EXPRESS YOURSELF: Go to *The Understanding Your Suicide Grief Journal* on p. 129.

HOW DO I KNOW IF I NEED PROFESSIONAL HELP?

It is not always easy to tell yourself you need professional help. Yet, if you are asking yourself this question and suspect you do need some help, go get it as soon as possible. The natural complications of suicide grief can affect your self-esteem, ability to trust, physical health, career, finances, and the list goes on. These are not insignificant matters and should not be ignored. Admitting you need some help is a sign of strength. A skilled professional can sometimes help facilitate the six needs of mourning (Touchstone Six) outlined in this book and affirm that you are doing the right things to help yourself heal.

Having encouraged anyone and everyone to seek counseling for this major life loss, do let me go over some "Red Flags" that indicate, I believe, that professional assistance is necessary:

- You feel stuck and time is passing without any sense of movement in your grief journey.

- You are experiencing deep depression that never eases up.

- You are having problems with anxiety, leaving you feeling immobilized (often accompanied by panic attacks).

- You are experiencing extensive "psychic numbing," where you feel you are watching yourself from the outside in.

189

- You are having profound sleep disturbances; difficulty getting any deep sleep leaves you feeling exhausted much of the time.

- You are not eating in a manner that allows you to maintain your weight; you are experiencing significant weight loss or gain.

- You feel an inability to provide basic care to yourself or your dependent children.

- You feel a profound sense of helplessness and hopelessness.

- You are having traumatic flashbacks to the scene of the suicide; you feel unable to take your mind off of the suicide even for brief periods of time.

- You feel like you never want to go out into the world; you are extremely withdrawn.

- You have a consistent pattern of real or imagined illness.

- You are overindulging in alcohol, drugs, food, or other addictive behaviors.

- You or others perceive that your behavior is high-risk and self-destructive, possibly including suicidal thoughts and plans.

Remember—it is a sign of strength to reach out and find a professional caregiver to support you during this time in which you are torn apart. You would probably go see a professional caregiver if you broke your leg, so why not consider seeing one when you have a broken heart? You deserve to have someone watch out for you right now and bear witness to you in ways that help you explore where you have been in life, where you are in life, and where you are going in life! Yes, mourning, by definition, requires the support of other people—"the shared social response to loss." Do not try to "handle" this by yourself. Acknowledge your vulnerability and find the compassionate help you deserve.

EXPRESS YOURSELF: Go to *The Understanding Your Suicide Grief Journal* on p. 130.

Medicating Yourself With Drugs, Alcohol, or Other Self-Destructive Behaviors

The pain that comes with the trauma of a death to suicide can result in some people consciously or unconsciously self-medicating the pain that must ultimately be embraced. As emphasized throughout this book, feelings will be integrated into your life only as they are expressed.

Therefore, you want to avoid self-treating your wounded soul with drugs, alcohol, or excessive behaviors that pull you off your path to healing. Some people who would not usually be vulnerable to abusing alcohol and drugs fall into this trap when a suicide death impacts their life. Unknowingly, this is often a path of self-destruction.

While you may be tempted to self-treat your pain away, doing so will only bring temporary relief from the pain of grief. Also, the sad reality is that the very thing that supplies what seems like relief has a life of its own. What may begin as an attempt to lessen pain eventually adds more pain. Inappropriate use of these chemicals increases tolerance, and soon more drugs or alcohol are needed to try to "manage" your emotional and spiritual anguish. WARNING: The use of prescription drugs, when appropriately prescribed and monitored, is very different from what I'm exploring with you here!

Remember—never take prescription drugs unless they were prescribed for you by a medical doctor. One major study found that many people get their first medication when they are in grief from well-meaning friends and family. Don't do it! You don't know how you might react to a certain medication.

Don't take a drug that your doctor has prescribed, either, unless you understand and agree with the reasons for taking it and the effects it will have on you. If you need more information about why you are being told to take any kind of medication, ASK! Drugs that make you feel numb or unnaturally peaceful will only complicate your grief experience. After all, they will eventually wear off and you will still have to struggle with the pain. If your doctor has prescribed a drug to help you cope with your grief, you may want to get a second opinion.

While some people try to self-treat their wounded soul with substances, others use excessive behaviors to numb their sorrow. Examples might include excess eating; premature replacement of the relationship; excess working; excess busyness; excess shopping (better know as "retail" therapy); excess exercise; excess caring for everyone else to the exclusion of self; excess risk-taking (such as gambling or driving under the influence of chemicals); excess traveling; and excess nicotine (after a death, some people start smoking, while existing smokers often increase this behavior—and yes, nicotine is a drug!).

One additional caveat here: Some people are predisposed to problems in this area because they tend to have what we call an "addictive personality." These people tend to over-engage with things they become involved with. This is where one drink leads to many more drinks; a little spending leads to a lot of spending; a little work leads to overwork; a little helping out others leads to codependent caretaking. You can probably discern if this description applies to you. If so, be aware of it and be on guard related to this tendency. What may on the surface seem like a form of temporary relief may result in huge additional chaos in your life. And if you reflect on this reality, you probably already have more than enough chaos going on surrounding your grief experience. Don't make yourself feel even crazier with these kinds of self-treating behaviors.

This is not to say that grieving people should never take medication. You may, for example, become so exhausted from lack of sleep that temporary use of a sedative is warranted. And in some situations, tranquilizers or antidepressants are appropriate therapies for severe emotional reactions to trauma. It is important to note that people who were taking antidepressants prior to the death of someone to suicide should continue taking them afterwards as ordered by a physician. Their grief will not be further complicated by the use of these medications. If it is suggested that you be on any medication related to your grief experience, I recommend that you combine that medication with ongoing counseling from a trained professional who is sensitive to the special needs of suicide survivors.

EXPRESS YOURSELF: Go to *The Understanding Your Suicide Grief Journal* on p. 130.

FRAMEWORK FOR CONSIDERATION OF GETTING PROFESSIONAL SUPPORT AND COUNSEL

A self-compassionate way to consider if you would benefit from professional support in your grief journey is to explore patterns that sometimes signal the need for help:

Postponing your grief: This is where you might find yourself delaying the expression of your grief, often hoping it will just go away. As you will come to know, it doesn't work that way. Traumatic grief will keep trying to get your attention until you give it the attention it demands. If you feel like you're putting off your grief in ways that are delaying your eventual healing, nudge yourself to go see a professional caregiver to at least explore this possibility.

Displacing your grief: This is where you, or people who care about you, see that you are in a pattern where you are taking the expression of your grief away from the actual loss and directing these intense feelings toward other things in your life. For example, you may find yourself hating every aspect of your work life; or you are always upset with your relationships with people around you; or you are cynical about life in general. If you recognize yourself in this pattern, go get some help and create momentum toward your healing.

Replacing you grief: This is when some people are prone to reinvesting prematurely in a new relationship after the loss of a significant relationship. While it is normal to want to feel loved after you have lost love, keep in mind that you are extremely vulnerable right now and probably lack discernment about which relationships are good for you and which are not. Also, realize that this replacement pattern does not only occur with other relationships, but potentially in other life activities as well. For example, you may over-invest in your work life to the exclusion of any leisure life. Unconsciously, this is often driven by the thought that if you keep busy, you won't feel the pain of your loss. Keep in mind that many people don't even consciously realize they have gotten into this replacement pattern of behavior. If you suspect this might have happened to you, do consider seeking some supportive counseling that can help redirect you to the genuine grief work that will ultimately help you heal.

Minimizing you grief: This is where you try to downplay the significance of your grief, thinking it is "no big deal." In other words, you are trying to prove to yourself that the loss in your life doesn't affect you very much. Or, you may keep trying to convince yourself about how "well you are doing" and want to think your life is "back to normal." Again, if you recognize yourself here, do consider some counseling to help you really see where you are in your grief journey.

Somaticizing your grief: This is where you feel sick all the time but your doctor can't find anything wrong with you. Essentially, this is when you convert your feelings of grief into physical symptoms. Some people get so completely preoccupied with their physical problems that they end up with little or no energy for other people or the work of mourning. Certainly, some physical symptoms often come with traumatic grief; however, what I'm describing here is where you have multiple physical symptoms, real or imagined, to the exclusion of befriending your need to mourn. Again, if you see any of yourself in this pattern, please get some supportive help from a well-trained, compassionate counselor.

In sum, the above patterns indicate you may well benefit from getting some additional help with your grief. The capacity to reach out for help can be a positive step in your personal development and a vitally important self-care need.

EXPRESS YOURSELF: Go to *The Understanding Your Suicide Grief Journal* on p. 131.

A FINAL WORD ABOUT REACHING OUT FOR HELP

As a grief counselor, I have been honored to companion hundreds of people who have been touched and changed when someone precious to them has taken his or her own life. Among the important lessons they have taught me is that sharing their grief with others is an integral part of the eventual healing process.

I truly hope this Touchstone has helped you understand the importance of reaching out for help during this season of your life. You need compassionate companions—fellow survivors, friends, family, and professional caregivers—who will walk with you and assure you that you need not walk alone through this wilderness experience.

Touchstone Nine

Seek Reconciliation, Not Resolution

"Unless you believe you are worthy of reconciliation and healing your suicide grief, you will question it, inhibit it, deny it, or push it away."

Alan D. Wolfelt

How do you ever find your way out of the wilderness of your grief? You don't have to dwell there forever, do you?

The good new is that no, you don't have to dwell there forever. If you follow the trail markers on your journey through the wilderness, you will find your way out. But just as with any significant experience in your life, the wilderness will always live inside you and be a part of who you are.

A number of psychological models describing grief refer to "resolution," "recovery," "reestablishment," or "reorganization" as being the destination of your grief journey. You may have heard—indeed you may believe—that your grief journey's end will come when you resolve, or recover from, your grief.

But you may also be coming to understand one of the fundamental truths of grief: Your journey will never truly end. People do not "get over" grief. My personal and professional experience tells me that a total return to "normalcy" after the death of someone loved is not possible; we are all forever changed by the experience of grief.

"Mourning never really ends. Only as time goes on, it erupts less frequently."
Anonymous

Reconciliation is a term I find more appropriate for what occurs as you work to integrate the new reality of moving forward in life without the physical presence of the person who died. With reconciliation comes a renewed sense of energy and confidence, an ability to fully acknowledge the reality of the death, and a capacity to become re-involved in the activities of living. There is also an acknowledgment that pain and grief are difficult, yet necessary, parts of life.

As the experience of reconciliation unfolds, you will recognize that life is and will continue to be different without the presence of the person who died. Changing the relationship with the person who died from one of presence to one of memory and redirecting one's energy and initiative toward the future often takes longer—and involves more hard work—than most people are aware. We, as human beings, never resolve our grief, but instead become reconciled to it.

"Truly, it is in the darkness that one finds the light, so when we are in sorrow then this light is nearest to all of us."
Meister Eckhart

We come to reconciliation in our grief journey when the full reality of the death becomes a part of us. Beyond an intellectual working through of the death, there is also an emotional and spiritual working through. What had been understood at the head level is now understood at the heart level.

Keep in mind that reconciliation doesn't just happen. You reach it through intentional mourning, by:

* talking it out.

* writing it out.

* crying it out.

* thinking it out.

* playing it out.

* painting (or sculpting, etc.) it out.

* dancing it out.

* etcetera!

To experience reconciliation requires that you *descend*, not *transcend*. You don't get to go around or above your grief. You must go through it. And while you are going through it, you must express it if you are to reconcile yourself to it.

Even the tragic suicide death of someone precious to you cannot take away your capacity to rediscover joy in your life. It may at times seem like events so conspire that you may lose sight of your capacity to experience happiness in life. In truth, your decision to slowly experience the reemergence of light in your life resides in you, whether you can see it or not. It's when you lose hope that you will ever be happy again that you must ask for compassionate people to companion you in this journey.

LEAP TOWARD YOUR HEALING

I realize that at times you may feel like you are crawling toward your healing; however, allow me to tell you a story about how sometimes you have to make LEAPS toward your healing.

A man had been walking near a cliff edge. He somehow got off the path, tripped, and fell over the edge. As he fell toward the ocean below, he grabbed a branch of thorns.

Dangling there, refusing to let go, the man began to pray, "Is there anybody there?" "Yes," came a reply. "Who is it?" inquired the man. "God." "Please help me God," prayed the man. "You have to let go and LEAP," said God. The man reflected on this for a moment, and then he prayed, "Is there anybody else there?"

Of course, the point of the story is that the man wants it both ways—he wants to hang on to the pain and also be free to go on with his life. Yet, he can't have it both ways, and neither can you. It is in integrating your pain and allowing it to soften over time that you ultimately allow peace and joy to re-enter your life. If you cling to your pain, you will never experience reconciliation.

However, if you do your grief work, the sharp, ever-present pain of grief will give rise to a renewed sense of meaning and purpose. Your feelings of loss will not completely disappear, yet they will soften, and the intense pangs of grief will become less frequent.

Hope for a continued life will emerge as you are able to make commitments to the future, realizing that the precious person who has taken his or her own life will never be forgotten. The unfolding of this journey is not intended to create a return to an "old normal" but the discovery of a "new normal."

EXPRESS YOURSELF: Go to *The Understanding Your Suicide Grief Journal* on p. 134.

To help you explore where you are in your movement toward reconciliation, the following signs that suggest healing may be helpful. You don't have to be seeing each of the signs for healing to be taking place. Again, remember that reconciliation is an ongoing process. If you are early in the work of mourning, you may not have found any of these signs yet in your journey. But this list will give you a way to monitor your movement toward healing. You may want to place checkmarks beside those signs you believe you are seeing.

SIGNS OF RECONCILIATION

As you embrace your grief and do the work of mourning, you can and will be able to demonstrate the majority of the following:

_____ A recognition of the reality and finality of the death.

_____ A return to stable eating and sleeping patterns.

_____ A renewed sense of release from the person who has died. You will have thoughts about the person, but you will not be preoccupied by these thoughts.

_____ The capacity to enjoy experiences in life that are normally enjoyable.

_____ The establishment of new and healthy relationships.

_____ The capacity to live a full life without feelings of guilt or lack of self-respect.

_____ The drive to organize and plan one's life toward the future.

_____ The serenity to become comfortable with the way things are rather than attempting to make things as they were.

_____ The versatility to welcome more change in your life.

_____ The awareness that you have allowed yourself to fully mourn and you have survived.

_____ The awareness that you do not "get over" your grief; instead, you have a new reality, meaning, and purpose in your life.

_____ The acquaintance of new parts of yourself that you have discovered in your grief journey.

_____ The adjustment to new role changes that have resulted from the loss of the relationship.

_____ The acknowledgment that the pain of loss is an inherent part of life resulting from the ability to give and receive love.

Reconciliation emerges much in the way grass grows. Usually we don't check our lawns daily to see if the grass is growing, but it does grow, and soon we come to realize it's time to mow the grass again. Likewise, we don't look at ourselves each day as mourners to see how we are healing. Yet we do come to realize, over the course of months and years, that we have come a long way. We have taken some important steps towards reconciliation.

"Reconciliation is not anchored in the absence of sadness; it is anchored in the intention to heal your sadness and renew your capacity to give and receive love."
Alan D. Wolfelt

Usually there is not one great moment of arrival, but rather subtle changes and small advancements. It's helpful to have gratitude for even very small steps forward. If you are beginning to taste your food again, be thankful. If you mustered the energy to meet your friend for lunch, be grateful. If you finally got a good night's sleep, rejoice.

One of my greatest teachers, C.S. Lewis, wrote in *A Grief Observed* about his grief symptoms as they eased in his journey to reconciliation:

"You are not alone, you are not to blame, and you are not doomed. You suffer as many others have, and like them you cannot only heal and continue to live, but you can enjoy life once again."
Ann Sonolin, John Guinan

There was no sudden, striking, and emotional transition. Like the warming of a room or the coming of daylight, when you first notice them they have already been going on for some time.

Of course, you will take some steps backward from time to time, but that is to be expected. Keep believing in yourself. Set your intention to reconcile your grief and have hope that you can and will come to live and love again.

SELF-CARE GUIDELINES

Movement toward your healing can be very draining and exhausting. As difficult as it might be, seek out people who give you hope for your healing. Permitting yourself to have hope is central to achieving reconciliation.

Realistically, even though you have hope for your healing, you should not expect it to happen overnight. Many grieving people think that it should and, as a result, experience a loss of self-confidence and self-esteem that leaves them questioning their capacity to heal. If this is the situation for you, keep in mind that you are not alone.

You may find that a helpful procedure is to take inventory of your own timetable expectations for reconciliation. Ask yourself questions like, "Am I expecting myself to heal more quickly than is humanly possible? Have I mistakenly given myself a specific deadline for when I should be 'over' my grief?" Recognize that you may be hindering your own healing by expecting too much of yourself. Take your healing one day at a time. It will ultimately allow you to move toward and rediscover continued meaning in your life.

One valuable way to embrace your healing is to use the journal that accompanies this book. Write down your many thoughts and feelings and you will be amazed at how it helps you embrace your grief. Having your experiences to reflect on in writing can also help you see the changes that are taking place in you as you do the work of mourning.

You can't control death or ignore your human need to mourn when it impacts your life. You do, however, have the choice to help yourself heal. Embracing the pain of your grief is probably one of the hardest jobs you will ever do. As you do this work, surround yourself with compassionate, loving people who are willing to walk with you.

EXPRESS YOURSELF: Go to *The Understanding Your Suicide Grief Journal* on p. 135.

HOPE FOR YOUR HEALING

The hope that comes from the journey through grief is life. The most important word in the previous sentence is *through*. As you do the work of mourning, you do not remain where you are.

"Hope is the feeling you have that the feeling you have isn't permanent."

Jean Kerr

Yes, you go to the wilderness, you cry out in the depths of your despair. Darkness may seem to surround you. But rising up within you is the profound awareness that the pain of grief is a sign of having given and received love. And where the capacity to love and be loved has been before, it can be again. Choose life!

Living in the present moment of your grief while having hope for a good that is yet to come are not mutually exclusive. Actually, hope and even anticipation can deepen your experience of the moment and motivate you to "work on!"

HOPE AND FAITH AS TRUST

In the Introduction to this book, I defined hope as an expectation of good that is yet to be. So, living with hope in the midst of your grief is living with anticipation that you can and will go on to discover a continued life that has meaning and purpose. If you are in any way like me, you may sometimes lose hope and need to fall back on your faith.

"You don't heal from the loss of a loved one because time passes, you heal because of what you do with the time."

Carol Crandell

Sometimes in my own grief journey, when hope seems absent, I open my heart—my well of reception—and find that it is faith that sustains me—faith that is inspired by the moments when I'm able to find what is good, what is sweet, what is tender in life, despite the deep, overwhelming wounds of my grief. It is the courage of the human spirit that chooses to live until we die that gives me faith. Life will continue, and it will bring me back to hope. If you lose hope along your journey, I invite you to join me in falling back on faith.

Reflect on this: Living with hope is living in anticipation of what can be. Sometimes when you are in the wilderness of your grief, it's easy to question your hope for the future. But living with faith is embracing what cannot be changed by our will, and knowing that life in all of its fullness is still good. Choose life!

HOPE AND FAITH IN GOD

In the religious traditions of Christianity and Judaism, hope is much more than an expectation of a good that is yet to be. Hope is confidence that God will be with you in your grief and, most important, that life continues after death. Hope is trust in God even when everything seems hopeless. Hope is the assurance that God has the last word, and that that word is LIFE—even as you confront the realities of the death of someone you have loved. Choose life!

EXPRESS YOURSELF: Go to *The Understanding Your Suicide Grief Journal* on p. 136.

A FINAL WORD ABOUT RECONCILIATION

The word *reconcile* comes from the Middle English for "to make good again." This is the essence of reconciliation in grief, actually—to make your life good again. You have the power to accomplish this. Through setting your intention to heal and intentional mourning, as well as reaching out for help from others, you can and will make your life good again.

In fact, in some ways, your life might be more than good—it might be richer and more deeply-lived. This transformative power of grief is the subject of the tenth and final Touchstone.

Touchstone Ten

Appreciate Your Transformation

*"Nature does not know extinction, all
it knows is transformation."*
Wernher Von Braun

The journey through the grief that follows the death of someone
precious to suicide is life-changing. When you leave the
wilderness of your grief, you are simply not the same person
as you were when you entered the wilderness. You have been
through so much. How could you be the same?

I'm certain you have discovered that you have been transformed
by your journey into grief. Transformation literally means an
entire change in form. Many mourners have said to me, "I have
grown from this experience. I am a different person." You are
indeed different now. Your inner form has changed. You have
likely grown in your wisdom, in your understanding, in your
compassion.

Now, don't take me the wrong way. Believe me, I understand
that the growth resulted from something you would have
preferred to avoid. Though grief can indeed transform into
growth, neither you nor I would seek out the pain of grief that

comes with a suicide death in an effort to experience this growth. While I have come to believe that our greatest gifts often come from our wounds, these are not wounds we masochistically go looking for. When others offer untimely comments like, "You'll grow from this," your right to be hurt, angry, or deeply sad is taken away from you. It's as if these people are saying that you should be grateful for the death! Of course you're not grateful for the death!

Someone you cared deeply about has taken his or her own life. You are a totally changed person. To understand how transformation in your grief occurs, let us explore some aspects of growth in grief.

EXPRESS YOURSELF: Go to *The Understanding Your Suicide Grief Journal* on p. 140.

GROWTH MEANS CHANGE

We as human beings are forever changed by the suicide death of someone in our lives. You may discover that you have developed new attitudes. You may be more patient or more sensitive to the feelings and circumstances of others, especially those suffering from loss. You may have new insights that guide the way you live your new life. You may have developed new skills or ways of viewing humankind or the world around you.

"Instead of recovery, the best I can hope for is an acceptance of how I have changed."

Edward K. Rynearson

You are "new," different than you were prior to the death. To the extent that you are different, you can say you have grown. Yes, growth means change.

EXPRESS YOURSELF: Go to *The Understanding Your Suicide Grief Journal* on p. 140.

GROWTH MEANS A NEW INNER BALANCE WITH NO END POINTS

While you may do your work of mourning in ways that help you recapture some sense of inner balance, it is a *new* inner balance. The word growth reflects that you do not reach some final end point in your grief journey.

None of us totally completes the mourning process. People who think you "get over" grief are often striving to pull it together while at the same time feeling that something is missing.

You don't return to a previous "inner balance" or "normal" but instead eventually achieve a new inner balance and a new normal. Yes, growth means a new inner balance.

EXPRESS YOURSELF: Go to *The Understanding Your Suicide Grief Journal* on p. 141.

GROWTH MEANS EXPLORING YOUR ASSUMPTIONS ABOUT LIFE

The death of someone to suicide invites you to look at your assumptions about life. Your loss experiences have a tendency to transform your assumptions, values, and priorities. What you may have thought of as being important—your nice house, your new car—may not matter any longer. The job or sport or financial goal that used to drive you may now seem trivial.

> *"Loss provides an opportunity to take inventory of our lives, to reconsider priorities, and to determine new directions."*
>
> Gerald L. Sittser

You may ask yourself, "Why did I waste my time on these things?" You may go through a rethinking or a transformation of your previously-held values. You may value material goods and status less. You may now more strongly value relationships.

As previously noted, when someone completes suicide, you may also find yourself questioning your religious and spiritual values. You might ask questions like, "How did God let this happen?" or

"Why did this happen to our family?" or "Why should I get my feet out of bed?"

Exploring these questions is a long and arduous part of the grief journey. But ultimately, exploring our assumptions about life can make these assumptions richer and more life-affirming. Every loss in life calls out for a new search for meaning, including a natural struggle with spiritual concerns, often transforming your vision of your God and your faith life. Yes, growth means exploring your assumptions about life.

"Finding meaning begins in questioning. Those who do not search, do not find."

Anonymous

EXPRESS YOURSELF: Go to *The Understanding Your Suicide Grief Journal* on p. 141.

GROWTH MEANS UTILIZING YOUR POTENTIAL

The grief journey often challenges you to reconsider the importance of using your potential. In some ways, death loss seems to free the potential within. Questions such as "Who am I? What am I meant to do with my life?" often naturally arise during grief. Answering them inspires a hunt. You may find yourself searching for your very soul.

In part, seeking purpose means living inside the question, "Am I making a living doing the work I love to do?" Beyond that, it means being able to affirmatively answer the question, "Does my life really matter?" Rather than dragging you down, your grief may ultimately lift you up. Then it becomes up to you to embrace and creatively express your newfound potential.

"Circumstances and situations do color life, but you have been given the mind to choose what the color should be."

John Homer Miller

Until you make peace with your purpose and using your potential, you may not experience contentment in your life. Joy will come to you when you know in your heart that you are using your potential—in your work or in your free time or in your relationships with friends and family.

I believe that grief's call to use your potential is why many mourners go on to help others in grief. You don't have to discover a cure for cancer. You may volunteer to help out with a suicide support group or a local hospice. You may reach out to a neighbor who is struggling or devote more time to your children or grandchildren. Remember—we all have gifts, and part of our responsibility is to discover what those gifts are and put them to use. Yes, growth means utilizing our potential.

EXPRESS YOURSELF: Go to *The Understanding Your Suicide Grief Journal* on p. 142.

YOUR RESPONSIBILITY TO LIVE

"Your joy is sorrow unmasked...

The deeper that sorrow carves into your being, the more joy you can contain.

When you are joyous, look deep into your heart and you shall find it is only that which has given you sorrow that is giving you joy.

When you are sorrowful, look again in your heart, and you shall see that in truth you are weeping for that which has been your delight."

Kahlil Gibran

Paradoxically, it is in opening to your broken heart that you open yourself to fully living until you die. You are on this earth for just a short time. You move through new developmental and spiritual stages daily, weekly, yearly.

Sorrow is an inseparable dimension of our human experience. We suffer after a loss because we are human. And in our suffering, we are transformed. While it hurts to suffer lost love, the alternative is apathy, which literally means the inability to suffer, and it results in a lifestyle that avoids human relationships to avoid suffering.

"Each day comes bearing its own gifts. Untie the ribbons."
Ruth Ann Schabaker

Perhaps you have noticed that some people die a long time before they stop breathing. They have no more promises to keep, no more people to love, no more places to go. It is as if the souls of these people have already died. Don't let this happen to you. Choose life!

Yes, you have to do your work of mourning and discover how you are changed. You have to live not only for yourself, but for the precious person in your life who has died—to work on his or her unfinished work and to realize his or her unfinished dreams. You can do this only by living.

Ask yourself: Am I doing something about the unfinished acts and dreams of the person who died? If you have in any way set your intention to live in pessimism and chronic sorrow, you are not *honoring* your grief, you are *dishonoring* the death.

I truly believe that those who have died live on through us, in our actions and deeds. When we honor their unfinished contributions to the living world, our dead live on. When we dedicate ourselves to helping others who come to know grief, they live on.

What if the person who died could return to see what you are doing with your life? What if he or she could see that you have mourned but also gone on to help others in grief and sorrow? What if he could see that he left his love forever in your heart? What if she could see that you live your life with passion in testimony to her? *No matter how deep your grief or how anguished your soul, bereavement does not free you from your responsibility to live until you die. The gift of life is so precious and fragile. Choose life!*

EXPRESS YOURSELF: Go to *The Understanding Your Suicide Grief Journal* on p. 142.

NOURISHING YOUR TRANSFORMED SOUL

Yes, your soul has been transformed by the suicide death of someone loved. Your soul is not a physical entity: it is everything about you that is not physical—your values, your identity, your memories, even your sense of humor. Naturally, grief work impacts your soul! I often say that grief work is soul work.

> *"I have been trying to make the best of grief and am just beginning to learn to allow it to make the best of me."*
>
> Barbara Lazear Ascher

In part, nourishing your grieving soul is a matter of surrendering to the mystery of grief. As I noted in the beginning of this book, real learning comes when we surrender: surrender our need to compare our grief (it's not a competition); surrender our self-critical judgments (we need to be self-compassionate); and surrender our need to completely understand (we never will). My hope is that the contents of this book have nourished your grieving soul.

There are, of course, many ways to nourish your grieving soul. Here are some that work for me. I nourish my soul...

- by attending to those things in life that give my life richness and purpose.

- by trying to fulfill my destiny, by developing my soul's potential.

- by striving to give back what others have given to me.

- by learning to listen to what is going on around and within me to help me decide which direction I need to go.

- by having gratitude for family and friends.

- by observing what is requesting my attention, and giving attention to it.

- by finding passion in ministering to those in grief.

- by going out into nature and having gratitude for the beauty of the universe.

- by praying that I'm living on purpose and using my gifts, whether by writing a book, teaching a workshop, or caring for my children.

- by setting aside time to go into exile and be by myself in stillness.

- by earning my living doing something I love to do.

- by going through my own struggles and griefs and realizing that it is working through these wounds that helps unite me with others.

How do you nourish your transformed soul? What can you do today and each and every day henceforth to pay homage to your transformation? How do you most authentically live your transformed life? These are the questions of your present and future life. It is in honoring these questions that you appreciate your transformation and live the best life you can.

"In the midst of winter, I found there was within me an invincible summer."
Albert Camus

EXPRESS YOURSELF: Go to *The Understanding Your Suicide Grief Journal* on p. 143.

CARRYING YOUR TRANSFORMATION FORWARD

Tomorrow is now. It is here. It is waiting for you. You have many choices in living the transformation that grief has brought to your life.

You can choose to visualize your heart opening each and every day. When your heart is open, you are receptive to what life brings you, both happy and sad. By "staying open," you create a gateway to your healing.

When this happens you will know that the long nights of suffering in the wilderness have given way to a journey towards the dawn. You will know that

"What a splendid way to move through the world... to bring our blessings to all that we touch."
Jack Kornfield

new life has come as you celebrate the first rays of a new light and new beginning. Choose life!

As you continue to experience how grief has transformed you, be open to the new directions your life is now taking. You have learned to watch for trail markers in your continued living. Listen to the wisdom of your inner voice. Make choices that are congruent with what you have learned on your journey. Say "YES" to life and "NO" to suicide. Bless you.

Contacts to Create Support Groups and Additional Resources

American Association of Suicidology (AAS)
5221 Wisconsin Avenue, NW
Washington, DC 20015
202-237-2280
www.suicidology.org

American Foundation for Suicide Prevention (AFSP)
120 Wall Street
New York, NY 10005
888-333-AFSP (2377)
www.afsp.org

Suicide Prevention Action Network USA (SPAN USA)
1025 Vermont Avenue, NW, Suite 1066
Washington, DC 20005
202-449-3600
www.spanusa.org

Center for Loss and Life Transition
3735 Broken Bow Rd.
Fort Collins, CO 80526
970-226-6050
www.centerforloss.com

For Immediate Help

National Suicide Prevention Lifeline
1-800-273-TALK (8255)
www.suicidepreventionlifeline.org

THE SUICIDE SURVIVOR'S BILL OF RIGHTS

Someone you love has ended his or her own life. Your grief is unique and profound, and you have special needs that must be tended to in the coming weeks, months, and years. Though you should reach out to others as you do the work of mourning, you should not feel obligated to accept the unhelpful responses you may receive from some people. You are the one who is grieving, and as such, you have certain "rights" no one should try to take away from you.

The following list is intended both to empower you to heal and to decide how others can and cannot help. This is not to discourage you from reaching out to others for help, but rather to assist you in distinguishing useful responses from hurtful ones.

1. **I have the right to experience my own unique grief.**
   No one else will grieve this death in exactly the same way I do. So, when I turn to others for help, I will not allow them to tell me what I should or should not be thinking, feeling, or doing.

2. **I have the right to talk about my grief.**
   Talking about my grief and the story of the death will help me heal. I will seek out others who will allow me to talk as much as I want, as often as I want, and who will listen without judging. If at times I don't feel like talking, I also have the right to be silent, although I understand that bottling everything up inside will prevent my healing.

3. **I have the right to feel a multitude of emotions.**
   Confusion, disorientation, fear, shame, anger, and guilt are just a few of the emotions I might feel as part of my grief journey. Others may try to tell me that what I do feel is wrong, but I know that my feelings aren't right or wrong, they just are.

4. **I have the right to work through any feelings of guilt and relinquish responsibility.**
   I may feel guilty about this death, even though it was in no way my fault. I must come to acknowledge that the only person truly responsible was the person who took his or her own life. Still, I must feel and explore any possible feelings of guilt I may have in order to move beyond them.

5. **I have the right to know what can be known about what happened.**
I can cope with what I know or understand, but it is much harder to cope with the unknown. If I have questions about the death, I have the right to have those questions answered honestly and thoroughly by those who may have the information I seek.

6. **I have the right to embrace the mystery.**
It is normal and natural for me to want to understand why the person I love took his or her own life, but I also have the right to accept that I may never fully and truly understand. I will naturally search for meaning, but I will also "stand under" the unknowable mystery of life and death.

7. **I have the right to embrace my spirituality.**
I will embrace and express my spirituality in ways that feel right to me. I will spend time in the company of people who understand and support my spiritual or religious beliefs. If I feel angry at God or find myself questioning my faith or beliefs, that's OK. I will find someone to talk with who won't be critical of my feelings of hurt and abandonment.

8. **I have the right to treasure my memories.**
Memories are one of the best legacies that exist after the death of someone loved. I will always remember. If at first my memories are dominated by thoughts of the death itself, I will realize that this is a normal and necessary step on the path to healing. Over time, I know I will be able to remember the love and the good times.

9. **I have the right to hope.**
Hope is an expectation of a good that is yet to be. I have the need and the right to have hope for my continued life. I can have hope and joy in my life and still miss and love the person who died.

10. **I have the right to move toward my grief and heal.**
Reconciling my grief will not happen quickly. Grief is a process, not an event. I will be patient and tolerant with myself and avoid people who are impatient and intolerant with me. I must help those around me understand that the suicide death of someone loved has changed my life forever.

If you have friends and family who want to support you in your grief but don't know how, feel free to photocopy this article for them. You'll also find a .pdf of the article on my website, www.centerforloss.com.

HELPING A SUICIDE SURVIVOR HEAL
by Alan D. Wolfelt, Ph.D.

Suicide and Silent Grief

Historian Arnold Toynbee once wrote, "There are always two parties to a death: the person who dies and the survivors who are bereaved." Unfortunately, many survivors of suicide suffer alone and in silence. The silence that surrounds them often complicates the healing that comes from being encouraged to mourn.

Because of the social stigma surrounding suicide, survivors often feel the pain of the loss yet may not know how, or where, or if, they should express it. Yet the only way to heal is to mourn. Just like other bereaved people grieving the loss of someone loved, suicide survivors need to talk, to cry, sometimes to scream, in order to heal.

As a result of fear and misunderstanding, survivors of suicide deaths are often left with a feeling of abandonment at a time when they desperately need unconditional support and understanding. Without a doubt, suicide survivors suffer in a variety of ways: one, because they need to mourn the loss of someone who has died; two, because they have experienced a sudden, typically unexpected traumatic death; and three, because they are often shunned by a society unwilling to enter into the pain of their grief.

Accept the Intensity of the Grief

Grief following a suicide is always complex. Survivors don't "get over it." Instead, with support and understanding, they can come to reconcile themselves to its reality. Don't be surprised by the intensity of their feelings. Sometimes when they least expect it, they may be overwhelmed by feelings of grief. Accept that survivors may be struggling with explosive emotions, guilt, fear, and shame well beyond the limits experienced in other types of death. Be patient, compassionate, and understanding.

Listen with Your Heart

Assisting suicide survivors means you must break down the terribly costly silence. Helping begins with your ability to be an active listener. Your physical presence and desire to listen without judgment are critical helping tools. Willingness to listen is the best way to offer help to someone who needs to talk.

Thoughts and feelings inside the survivor may be frightening and difficult to acknowledge. Don't worry so much about what you will say. Just concentrate on the words that are being shared with you.

Your friend may relate the same story about the death over and over again. Listen attentively each time. Realize this repetition is part of your friend's healing process. Simply listen and understand. And remember, you don't have to have an answer.

Avoid Simplistic Explanations And Clichés

Words, particularly clichés, can be extremely painful for a suicide survivor. Clichés are trite comments often intended to diminish the loss by providing simple solutions to difficult realities. Comments like, "You are holding up so well," "Time will heal all wounds," "Think of what you still have to be thankful for," and "You have to be strong for others" are not constructive. Instead, they hurt and make a friend's journey through grief more difficult.

Be certain to avoid passing judgment or providing simplistic explanations of the suicide. Don't make the mistake of saying the person who completed suicide was "out of his or her mind." Inappropriate judging only complicates the suicide survivor's grief. Instead, suicide survivors need help in coming to their own search for understanding of what has happened. In the end, their personal search for meaning and understanding of the death is what is really important.

Be Compassionate

Give your friend permission to express his or her feelings without fear of criticism. Learn from your friend. Don't instruct or set explanations about how he or she should respond. Never say, " I know just how you feel." You don't. Think about your helping role as someone who "walks with," not behind or in front of the one who is grieving.

Familiarize yourself with the wide spectrum of emotions that many survivors of suicide experience. Allow your friend to experience all the hurt, sorrow, and pain that he or she is feeling at the time. And recognize tears are a natural and appropriate expression of the pain associated with the loss.

Respect the Need to Grieve

Often ignored in their grief are the parents, brothers, sisters, grandparents, aunts, uncles, spouses, and children of people who have taken their own lives. Why? Because of the nature of the death, it is sometimes kept a secret. If the death cannot be talked about openly, the wounds of grief will go unhealed.

As a caring friend, you may be the only one willing to be with the survivors. Your physical presence and permissive listening create a foundation for the healing process. Allow the survivors to talk, but don't push them. Sometimes you may get a cue to back off and wait. If you get a signal that this is what is needed, let them know you are ready to listen if, and when, they want to share their thoughts and feelings.

Use the name of the person who has died when talking to survivors. Hearing the name can be comforting, and it confirms that you have not forgotten this important person who was so much a part of your friend's life.

Understand the Uniqueness of Suicide Grief

Keep in mind that the grief of suicide survivors is unique. No one will respond to the death of someone loved in exactly the same way. While it may be possible to talk about similar phases shared by survivors, everyone is different and shaped by experiences in his or her life.

Because the grief experience is unique, be patient. The process of grief takes a long time, so allow your friend to proceed at his or her own pace. Don't criticize what you may think is inappropriate behavior. Remember that the death of someone to suicide is a shattering experience. As a result of this death, your friend's life is under reconstruction.

Be Aware of Holidays and Anniversaries

Survivors of suicide may have a difficult time on special occasions like holidays and anniversaries. These events emphasize the absence of the person who has died. Respect this pain as a natural expression of the grief process. Learn from it. And most important, never try to take the hurt away.

Be Aware of Support Groups

Support groups are one of the best ways to help survivors of suicide. In a group, survivors can connect with other people who share the commonality of the experience. They are allowed and encouraged to tell their stories as much, and as often, as they like. You may be able to help survivors locate such a group. This practical effort on your part will be appreciated.

Respect Faith and Spirituality

If you allow it, a survivor of suicide will teach you about his or her feelings regarding faith and spirituality. If faith is a part of her life, let her express it in ways that seem appropriate. If he is mad at God, encourage him to talk about it. Remember, having anger at God speaks of having a relationship with God. Don't be a judge; be a loving friend.

Survivors may also need to explore how religion may have complicated their grief. They may have been taught that people who take their own lives are doomed to hell. Your task is not to explain theology but to listen and learn. Whatever the situation, your presence and desire to listen without judging are critical helping tools.

Work Together as Helpers

Friends and family who experience the death of someone loved to suicide must no longer suffer alone and in silence. As helpers, you need to join with other caring people to provide support and acceptance for survivors, who need your help mourning in healthy ways.

To experience grief is the result of having loved. Suicide survivors must be guaranteed this necessity. Helping a suicide survivor may not be an easy task. You may have to give more concern, time, and love than you ever knew you had. But this effort will be more than worth it.

Acknowledgments

In my years as a grief companion and educator, I have had the honor of walking with hundreds of people journeying through the wilderness of suicide grief. They have shared their lives, their losses, and their healing with me in ways that have deeply touched me and forever changed my life.

Without their willingness to teach me, this book would not be, nor would I be who I am. I want to thank each and every person who has been willing to talk openly and honestly about their intimate stories of suicide with me. It is through you that these pages have unfolded.

I would like to thank my caring and compassionate staff at the Center for Loss and Life Transition for how they keep the Center focused on our vision of "helping people help others" during the times I'm away in exile writing a book to help people on their healing paths. Your support, understanding and passion for what we do at our healing center are invaluable to me. I also thank the fine folks in the Virgin Islands and mountains of Colorado who nurtured me while I was in retreat penning this book.

To my friends Nan and Gary Zastrow from Wausau, Wisconsin for their willingness to read the first draft of this book and make invaluable suggestions that helped improve the content... a heartfelt thank you. Also, thanks for helping me get to know your precious son, Chad. His spirit is alive in the pages of this book.

I also thank my editor, Karla, for her intelligence, sensitivity to this important topic, and heart in guiding my books into the light of day.

To my family for the love and nurturance you provide me each and every day. A special thanks to my wonderful daughter Megan, who took my terrible handwriting and input my words into computer language. I will always remember that you and I worked together on this important resource in hopes that it would help thousands of people mourn well, so they could go on to live well and love well!

To contact Dr. Wolfelt and for information on his books and
workshops, please write, call, or e-mail:

Alan Wolfelt
Center for Loss and Life Transition
3735 Broken Bow Road
Fort Collins, CO 80526
970-226-6050
www.centerforloss.com

DrWolfelt@centerforloss.com

The Understanding Your Suicide Grief Journal

Exploring the Ten Essential Touchstones

For many people, journaling is an excellent way to process their many painful thoughts and feelings after a death. While private and independent, journaling is still the outward expression of grief. And is is through the outward expression of grief that we heal.

ISBN 978-1-879651-59-3 • 136 pages • softcover • $14.95

The Understanding Your Suicide Grief Support Group Guide

Meeting Plans for Facilitators

This book is for those who want to facilitate an effective suicide grief support group. It includes 12 meeting plans that interface with *Understanding Your Suicide Grief* and its companion journal.

ISBN 978-1-879651-60-9 • 44 pages • softcover • $12.95

The Wilderness of Suicide Grief

Finding Your Way

A beautiful, hardcover gift book version of *Understanding Your Suicide Grief*

This excerpted version of *Understanding Your Suicide Grief* makes an excellent gift for anyone grieving the suicide death of someone loved. This is an ideal book for the bedside or coffee table. Pick it up before bed and read just a few pages. You'll be carried off to sleep by its gentle, affirming messages of hope and healing.

ISBN 978-1-879651-68-5 • hardcover • 128 pages • $15.95